Living with Health Issues

Richard Weaver

chipmunkapublishing
the mental health publisher

All rights reserved, no part of this publication may be reproduced by any means, electronic, mechanical photocopying, documentary, film or in any other format without prior written permission of the publisher.

Published by
Chipmunkapublishing
United Kingdom

http://www.chipmunkapublishing.com

Copyright © 2016 Richard Weaver

ISBN   978-1-78382-273-7

Forward - Page 5
Part One - Introduction
Chapter 1 - "In A Muddle" - Page 7
Chapter 2 - Search For Answers - Page 13
Chapter 3 - What Next? - Page 15

Part Two - Mental Health Act 1983
Chapter 4 - General Notes On Being 'Sectioned' - Page 17
Chapter 5 - Compulsory Detention of Informal Patients and Emergency Admission for Assessment - Page 21
Chapter 6 - Admission for Assessment (Section 2) - Page 23
Chapter 7 - Admission for Treatment (Section 3) - Page 25
Chapter 9 - Removal of Patient by Police (Sections 135 or 136) - Page 27

Part Three - Mental Health Act 1983 - Criminally Detained Patients
Chapter 9 - Court Remands (Sections 35 or 36) - Page 29
Chapter 10 - Hospital Order (Section 37) - Page 31
Chapter 11 - Interim Hospital Order (Section 38) - Page 33
Chapter 12 - Hospital Order With Restrictions (Sections 37 & 41) - Page 35
Chapter 13 - Transfer From Prison (Sections 48 & 49 and 47 & 49) - Page 37

Part Four - Mental Health Act 1983 (Community Sections)
Chapter 14 - Guardianships (Section 7) - Page 39
Chapter 15 - Community Treatment Order (Section 17a) - Page 41

Part Five - Protecting Yourself In The Community
Chapter 16 - What Is Abuse? - Page 43
Chapter 17 - Being Targeted For Being 'Different' - Page 45
Chapter 18 - Strangers Trying To Take Advantage of You - Page 49
Chapter 19 - "Fair-Weather Friends" - Page 51
Chapter 20 - Sexual Exploitation - Page 55
Chapter 21 - True Friends - Page 57
Chapter 22 - Agencies Who Can Stop You Being Abused - Page 59

Part Six - Self Help
Chapter Twenty-Three - Nobody Can Do It For You - Page 61
Chapter Twenty-Four - You Can't Do It Alone Either - Page 65
Chapter Twenty-Five - Resources Available - Page 67
Chapter Twenty-Six - Crisis Teams - Page 71
Chapter 27 - Using Your Condition Against Itself - Page 73
Chapter 28 - Appropriate Use of PRN Medication - Page 75
Chapter 29 - Keeping Busy - Page 77

Part Seven - Employment With A Diagnosis
Chapter 30 - Voluntary Work - Page 79
Chapter 31 - Gaining Qualifications - Page 83
Chapter 32 - If You Have A Criminal Record - Page 87
Chapter 33 - Applying For Unpaid Work - Page 89
Chapter 34 - When to 'Come Clean' About Your Medical History - Page 91
Chapter 35 - Choosing Suitable Work - Page 93

Part Eight - Community Care
Chapter 36 - Differences Between Nursing Homes and Residential Care Homes - Page 95
Chapter 37 - Which Is Right For You? - Page 97
Chapter 38 - Funding Application - Page 99
Chapter 39 - Complaints - Page 101
Chapter 40 - Advocates - Page 103
Chapter 41 - The Care Quality Commission - Page 105
Chapter 42 - The Mental Capacity Act - Page 107
Chapter 43 - Miscellaneous - Page 109

Forward

As a person who lives with Asperger's syndrome (a social and communication disorder on the autistic spectrum), psychosis, mood disorder and a number of lesser mental health problems, I have first-hand experience of the subject. I therefore decided it was time to write about how I originally received inaccurate diagnoses, the struggles both I and my family went through in order to get the correct diagnosis, and then appropriate treatment. In the pages that follow I will talk about how these problems have affected my day to day life in childhood, adolescence, and adulthood (although this will not involve a short autobiography). I hope this project will enable (assuming it gets completed) the reader with psychiatric problems to understand you are not 'crazy' or 'beyond help' and you DO have a future. Whilst (as I have found) you may never eradicate your symptoms completely or even very much, that doesn't mean in any way you can't or shouldn't lead a full, satisfying and meaningful life.

You may (as I have) been in trouble with the police, maybe for serious offences - this isn't the end of the world. I have twice been convicted of attempted robbery (and on the first occasion possession of a replica firearm too) -it hasn't stopped me getting part-time paid employment with CHOICE (the organisation who own and the care home where I currently reside) carrying out home inspections in other CHOICE homes in the area to the tune of about £10 per hour.

Again, having spent time in secure units in the past need not mean always being dependent on the system, or even after leaving hospital never being very independent. Less than five years ago I was in a secure unit, and had to be accompanied by two staff at first. In the last five weeks I've TWICE flown from Southampton to Edinburgh totally unsupported.

For those who work in branches of mental health care, I hope this resource will also be useful by providing an insight first-hand into the isolation having both mental illnesses and a developmental disorder can cause. As stated in the above paragraphs, care-workers will be able to see the transition it is possible for a person affected by poor mental health given the necessary resources, expertise, patience, support from family and friends, time, self-belief and an unshakeable desire to succeed come what may.

Of course for carers of other disciplines this work may be useful. Suppose a patient from a psychiatric hospital (voluntary or sectioned) or someone more advanced in their treatment who is living in a residential care home (or even a prisoner under escort who has mental health problems) needs admission to a casualty department in a general hospital (which may even lead to transfer to another general ward) or directly to one of the other wards - if the doctors and nurses caring for this person understand some of his or her mental problems, it follows the patient can be given better care. Imagine someone experiencing a chronic psychosis is admitted to a general ward, they are likely to be more disruptive than the majority of people being looked after there. Whilst it is true that if someone was already seriously mentally ill when their physical illness or accident occurred, they would almost certainly be supported anyway - this doesn't alter the fact that if staff in the general hospital in question had a reasonable understanding of why the patient was being disruptive - it would be easier to be sympathetic and also reassure other patients who may find this disturbing.

For friends and relatives of anybody affected by mental health problems, if they may be worried the particular patient is being mistreated in a psychiatric hospital; or worried their friend or relative may never recover or get a job - I hope this project will offer constructive advice.

Finally, for anyone else who is curious about the subject, or maybe studying mental health nursing or psychiatry as an intended career; and yes, I hope this project will one day make me a few 'readies'.

Richard Weaver October 2014

Part One - Introduction

Chapter 1 - "In a muddle"

In the depth of mental distress, it is hard to know whether you are 'coming or going'! If hearing strange voices inside (or even outside) your head, seeing 'visions' (apparent 3D images in front of you, that are out of place with your surroundings; Darth Vader in the middle of a field would be a good case in point) or hold beliefs that just about everyone you know regards as 'weird' - it is easy to assume you are 'cracking up'. I know when I was 16, and cycling to the restaurant where I worked at the time, it was broad daylight and to this day (I'm now 42) I can remember seeing an image of a full-sized lorry flying about 80 to 90 feet above the trees on the left-hand side of the dual carriageway. I really, truly thought I had started on the road to 'madness'. For what it's worth, I now know that the word 'madness' is a meaningless, derogatory and totally unhelpful word used by ignorant people to describe fellow human beings who experience unusual or inexplicable phenomena, but that's another story...

Mental illness often manifests fully in the patient's late teens or early twenties, but even years earlier (say at primary school) he or she will often be regarded by peers (and to a lesser extent teachers and parents) as 'oddballs' and thus be far more vulnerable than the average pupil to bullying both physically and psychologically (of course the much intensified degree of bullying meted out only goes to exacerbate the degree of mental illness when the person later becomes obviously ill).

I certainly had to put up with more than my fair share of this throughout my entire school career, and it didn't end when I went out to work. A good case in point of bullying at work occurred in the small hours of the morning on New Year's Day 1989, whilst a staff New Year party at the restaurant I mentioned a couple of paragraphs ago. Anyway, other staff members present (male and female) held me down and whipped my boxer shorts down. If it happened at the age I am now, I would certainly see the funny side of - hell, a few months ago I took part in a charity bike lasting 2 hours with NOTHING on, and half the men and women in Portsmouth saw what I've; but at age 16 to have penis and testicles exposed to half-a-dozen young women (like most lads that age I was convinced I had the small penis on the planet) humiliated me to the point that I very nearly resigned from my job, had it not been for my Mum and Dad persuading at length to retract the resignation I would have gone through with it - and then had no job.

Owing to the fact I have Asperger's syndrome as well psychosis this caused me to endure additional bullying at school for three main reasons; firstly, having the condition inevitably caused me to display very poor social skills (remember Asperger's is a social and communication disorder), secondly Asperger's is often associated with dyspraxia (the medical condition of clumsiness) and this is certain true of me, consequently I'm not good at sport and therefore had the 'rise' taken with little let-up, and until I began weight training in the 5th year, I was very physically weak (even relatively to my then tiny frame) so physical bullying was easy for others to inflict and impossible for me to defend against - and didn't the other kids just love it that way, knowing I couldn't do a thing about it, and also knowing that I was fully aware that they knew I was stymied - it must of given those young lads such a feeling of control and power.

Psychiatric patients who end up in prison (even if only on remand) often discover that their mental health state rapidly deteriorates even if only mildly unwell when originally sent to jail. Officers who work in prisons have little or no mental health training, even on the healthcare wing - admittedly, prison warders get considerably better mental health training than in years gone by, however great investment in training prison staff is still needed, which requires funding, staff and governors to research into why prisoners with mental health problems fair so badly, and introduce Occupational Therapy, and CBT (Cognitive Behavioural Therapy) and in any event, on the healthcare wing (in common with general population) prisoners are held in cells which they lack interaction, they end up severely bored. As if this wasn't enough psychiatric patients tend be heavy smokers, and of course, inside, inmates simply don't have the money.

In terms of the essential mental health training of the officers and implementing therapy programmes are concerned; there just isn't the money. For this reason the authorities try to ensure prisoners with psychiatric needs are "sectioned" to hospital either via the courts or preferably, directly under the Ministry of Justice (using prison transfer powers). A prisoner admitted to hospital by this method, will automatically be taken to the hospital straight from jail, escorted by the officers.

A major problem encountered by people admitted to psychiatric wards (especially locked ones) is that invariably some of the other patients they are thrown in with (and if a locked ward, locked in with) are going to be acutely unwell and continually displaying either physically and/ or verbally aggressive conduct and/ or other untoward behaviour. When someone is in hospital and suffering severe emotional distress, and other patients around them are acting in this sort of disruptive way, the atmosphere can feel unbearable. If the person concerned is detained on a locked ward and does not even have supported leave of absence (I don't like the term 'escorted' - it sounds too custodial) he or she has no means of getting away from the environment. In a situation involving serious physical violence it wouldn't help even if the patient had supported leave, as in practice, the very time it would be helpful to leave the ward to 'get some peace and quiet' staff would to be too busy dealing with the violent occurrence. Furthermore, in this same situation, because all staff resources have to be pooled to cope with the current incident, they are not going to be available to talk to or otherwise reassure other patients who may be terrified by the events they are witnessing.

The good news is, when a patient is getting better, leave increases through supported and the unsupported and in time, there is opportunity for transfer to a non-secure ward. If the patient is voluntary they would be cared for on an open ward automatically and would have the legal right to come and go as they pleased - supported or unsupported simply wouldn't come in to it. The one possible exception where a patient requests support on a particular occasion owing to specific worries or issues that time and provided a member of staff is available to accompany that person. At any rate, for the detained patient, once well enough to reside on an unlocked ward the 'challenging behaviour' inevitably encountered on a locked one, although it will doubtless occur, the frequency and severity would normally be considerably less.

Regrettably, another problem many patients held in secure wards face is 'heavy-handedness' to greater or lesser degrees, by staff themselves. Having been in a few such places myself I have both witnessed and been on the receiving end of it myself, not to mention heard some pretty bad reports from former patients of other secure institutions, when patients remonstrate (kick-off in plain English) this is often met by excessive restraint, forced injections (with the patient quite literally having their underwear forcibly pulled down and being injected in the backside). I have both seen (and heard from patient's previously held in places such as Broad moor) patients being denied the right to smoke for hours at a time as a punishment when their behaviour is deemed unacceptable. I remember once when I was on locked ward in Salisbury, one of the female patients being denied a cigarette for 24 hours merely for refusing to attend Industrial Therapy (the hospital factory, where some patients worked for a maximum incentive payment of £5 per week).

I have personally been a victim of a male nurse deliberately twisting my wrist in a restraint even after I stopped struggling, and the force exerted almost result in the bone breaking! Quite apart from the fact this sort of behaviour on part of staff is grossly disproportionate, and frankly cruel, by very virtue of patients being detained in hospital because they lack responsibility for their own actions; it therefore follows that punishment is not appropriate. Of course staff abusing service users does not stop at secure units - Winterbourne House in Bristol being a good case in point. Incidentally, I don't mean to be all doom and gloom; there are, thankfully, good care homes, good psychiatric wards and yes pleasant, friendly and caring nurses who work on locked wards. I am just trying to paint a realistic picture of what someone might experience during the early days of treatment.

Although I am going to talk about medication in more detail later, I'm just going to raise a few general points: firstly it should be clearly understood that medication will not 'cure' your mental illness, as such. It does (in about 30% of cases) totally suppress symptoms of psychosis or schizophrenia while the patient continues to take it as directed by his or her doctor, but if he or she ever discontinues taking it, the symptoms will almost certainly return. The next thing to consider is that sometimes it can literally take years to respond to treatment. Of course, as should be evident from the contents pages, medication is only one of a variety of interventions (treatments) that will need to be used together to facilitate the path to your recovery (recovery, of course doesn't have to mean being 'well' in the clinical sense of the word - as I pointed out in the forward it is quite possible to live a relatively independent life even in the presence of quite severe symptoms). Also, all medications do cause side-effects, ranging from a dry mouth to so-called 'lock-jaw' or involuntary limb movements. Just about any anti-psychotic drug will make you slightly lethargic and probably cause weight-gain. In the case of anti--depressants (unlike anti-psychotics) these are normally only prescribed for short term use, and as long as weaned off in a controlled manor, the chances are that the depressive illness won't come back. For problems like OCD (Obsessive Compulsive Disorder) anti-depressants (in particular Prozac) may be prescribed more or less on a permanent basis, as they seem to alleviate obsessive thoughts. The likely reason that this treatment works is that someone with an OCD basically never feels 'good enough' hence they are always 'raising the bar' and the effects of an anti-depressant help negate their feelings of low self-worth. OCD does in-fact, have a positive side (namely a natural inclination to always give 200%) and therefore can make OCD patients (at least in some respects) attractive to employers. The down side being, speaking from personal experience, that as the illness gets a tighter and tighter grip, you increasingly get sucked ever deeper into being a perfectionist, and the point is bound to be reached when you can no longer achieve your own goals, and thus feel a failure. I know from being in this position to greater or lesser degrees myself, for most of my adult life, you just grit your teeth, try harder and harder, you become exhausted, irritable and depressed, and furthermore you may judge others by your own ultra-high standards.

Personally, although I do judge others by my own standards, I give others far more leeway than I give myself. Perfectionists are invariably their own worst critics by far!

The common symptoms (or features) of schizophrenic type illness include hallucinations (especially **auditory** hallucinations, namely hearing voices) or (**visual** hallucinations, like the vision of the flying lorry I had age 16) or another possible symptom could be to suffer delusions (fully believing something that 99.9% of people know to be impossible, such as if I genuinely believed I was Julius Ceaser, that would be a delusion) or another common symptom experienced by psychiatric patients may be paranoia (gross mistrust of others with no basis for that distrust) or a fourth problem arises when people believe they are getting messages from TV or radio. Messages from the TV or radio are not 'external hallucinations' seeming to emanate from the TV or radio (as the case maybe) when switched off; but rather when a broadcast is in progress, an unusual personal interpretation of normal day to day TV and radio programmes.

Richard Weaver

Chapter 2 – Search for Answers

The obvious person to talk to is your GP. If he/ she thinks necessary, you can be referred to a psychiatrist or psychologist. If you are awaiting trial for an offence (either on bail or on remand) and you feel you need professional help with your offending, as you are having serious problems controlling your criminal behaviour owing to your current mental health state, it is vital you inform your legal representative (solicitor). Your solicitor can arrange for a psychiatric assessment at your health centre or other suitable location (possibly at home) or if you are in custody the doctors will of course visit the prison and assess you there. If you are in prison, and have (or at least likely to have) a mental disorder, you will probably be housed on the healthcare wing. The prison psychiatrist (doctor) may recommend you receive medications whilst detained in prison, although unless it is an emergency you CANNOT be forced to receive them.

Another (quite different) emergency situation which could urgent assessment would be admission to an Accident and Emergency Department as a result of an obviously determined suicide attempt. You will certainly be seen by a member of the local crisis team, and may well be offered informal admission to hospital to receive treatment for a depressive illness. You don't have to agree, but if you do refuse you can, if the relevant criteria apply, be compelled to go into hospital anyway to prevent you from making further attempts on your own life. If you are offered voluntary admission and refuse, your right to do so has to be respected by law.

If you are admitted as a voluntary patient or consent to informal admission you will have the legal right to leave the ward for shopping or any other purpose. However, if the admission is an informal one rather than voluntary, a nurse or doctor can put a hold on you if it is felt your leaving the ward at that time could endanger you, a member of the public or both.

In a situation, where a psychiatrist, having received a non-urgent referral from your GP, nonetheless feels that you could benefit from treatment, you can be offered either outpatient treatment. This means remaining in your own home and you would continue with your normal daily routine of work, college or whatever you normally do, but may attend a support group, and of course you would have appointments with your psychiatrist from time to time. If you are not currently employed in the paid or voluntary sector or at college/ in training, you may be asked to attend Industrial Therapy at a local hospital. You will be paid small amounts for the work, and travel expenses are covered.

Attendance will probably be a condition of treatment, you can of course decline - but if you do, you risk being discharged from the psychiatrist's care. This would also apply to community treatments in general.

If your psychiatrist doesn't think you are a risk to yourself or anyone else but does think you are unwell enough to need care in hospital you can be offered voluntary admission but CANNOT be forced to be admitted. You may choose to discharge yourself at any time of the day or night - staff MUST respect this: If you do choose to discharge yourself against medical advice, you can be required to sign a disclaimer agreeing the hospital are not responsible if anything goes majorly wrong. Furthermore you CANNOT be made to receive any medications or treatments you do not want, however if you regularly refuse treatment it will probably be viewed that nothing will be achieved by you remaining in hospital, and you will therefore be discharged. You can also be discharged if involved in an incident of serious misconduct or violence, and the police may well be called.

If you are a voluntary patient and there is a major change of circumstance, you may be regraded as informal (meaning you are not obliged to stay in hospital by law but you are effectively coerced in to doing so). As such, if you then attempted to discharge yourself (or take temporary leave from hospital against medical advice) you then be held on a short term section (a section is a clause of the Mental Health Act that allows you to be kept in hospital against you will). This is explained in greater detail, later.

Chapter 3 – What next?

Suppose you are seen by a psychiatrist in the community, and either he or she thinks you do not have a mental illness or disorder/ learning difficulty, but he or she feels you do need other kinds of help e.g. psychological treatments or placement in a "Half-way house" or residential care home/ group home, a funding application will be made by a social worker for payment of living costs. The cost will probably be split between your Primary Care Trust (this is the NHS Trust responsible for the care of all NHS patients in the part of the country you reside or your parents reside) and your local social services. There is a minimum period of time that either you or your parents must live in a particular place to come under the responsibility of a particular PCT or Social Services Department. If you or your parents have lived there less than the statutory minimum, the rules for establishing who is responsible for funding care becomes more complex.

For schizophrenia, and similar illness (and for alleviating anxiety associated with conditions untreatable in themselves - such as the Asperger's syndrome I have to live with) there are numerous types of 'anti-psychotic' drugs available. The first drug of this type ever invented (in the 1950s) was Chlorpromazine (also known as Largactil). Interestingly enough, this particular drug was developed as an anti-emetic (anti-sickness drug). Whilst Chlorpromazine performs its originally intended function perfectly well, by chance, it was discovered that Chlorpromazine acts as an effective tranquiliser (anxiety relief drug) and for some patients it also reduces or even completely suppresses their symptoms (but as I pointed out on page 10, the medication will not cure the symptoms per se). Another fairly old anti-psychotic drug is Stelazine; newer ones include Olanzapine, and Clozapine.

Many drugs perform more than one function (I've mentioned Chlorpromazine "Doubling-up as an anti-sickness and an anti-psychotic, and I've also mentioned Prozac being used to treat OCD as well as depression) but there are many other examples; to name few: Sodium Valporate (an anti-epileptic drug) can also be used as a mood stabiliser; or again a number of anti-depressants can be used in part of the treatment of Anorexia Nervosa (compulsive crash dieting) and certain anti-depressants are prescribed that "Double-up" to reduce/ stop psychotic symptoms.

How, you might ask, do the medications actually 'dampen-down' psychotic symptoms such as hearing voices or sounds, seeing images that others don't etc?

The answer lies in two main facts: (1) I have already pointed out that these medications are tranquilisers, and as such, by lowing anxiety levels make you less aware of the intrusive voices, visions and so which calms them further, reducing the voices even more. In other words, this creates a positive circle (2) the medications correct chemical in the brain called neuro-transmitters which are responsible for conveying messages from the eyes, ears etc to the brain, for interpretation. In psychosis, too much of this chemical is produced resulting in garbled messages the brain attempts to translate, which become 'decoded' as 'visions' or 'voices' and so on. The drugs (assuming the dosage is correct) should correct the level of the neuro-transmitters to an optimum value, thus 'knocking out' these strange experiences.

Indirectly, this can also be useful for controlling delusions. As I explained, a delusion is essentially a bizarre belief, and if you experienced delusions, although not always the case, a common reason you may suffer from them would be the result of being "Brain-washed" into believing the particular thoughts suggested by 'voices' that appear to talk you (assuming you hear voices) It therefore follows that if the 'voices' can eradicated (or least significantly reduced) by the medication, the 'knock-on' effect will be, that his or her delusions should diminish. It has been suggested that some people suffer delusions originating from voices they don't even realise they hear.

Part Two - Mental Health Act 1983
(General notes on being 'sectioned' and civilly detained patients)

Chapter 4 - General notes on being 'sectioned'

To be held under The Mental Health Act, you must suffer (or for an assessment section might reasonably suffer) from what the Act refers to as Mental Disorder combined with behaviour that puts you and/ or others at risk, and where there is a clear correlation (relationship) between the two.

There are four types of mental disorder as defined in Section 1

1. Mental Illness
There is no clear definition under The Act of what Mental Illness means. The Act states (more or less) that mental illness is a matter for clinical decision by the consultant concerned.

2. Mental Impairment
The Mental Health defines this as a state of /arrested intelligence or incomplete development of the mind' combined with 'abnormally aggressive behaviour'. The essential clause of 'abnormally aggressive behaviour' is used so that although the person's /arrested intelligence or incomplete development of the mind' will itself never alter, if the 'abnormally aggressive behaviour' itself can be corrected, it prevents the situation arising whereby those with low intellect or other learning disability automatically spend the rest of their lives' on section.

3. Severe Mental Impairment
This is defined as 'arrested intelligence or incomplete development of the mind to a severe degree' associated with abnormally aggressive behaviour to a degree markedly worse than within the Mental Impairment definition. Similarly, as the person progresses, hopefully the heightened level of aggression moves down to the degree typical of mental impairment, in turn this comes under enough control that the aggressive behaviour is sufficiently diminished to enable the 'aggression clause' to no longer apply and the person free to live as he or she chooses.

4. Psychopathic Disorder
Arguably, psychopathic disorder is not an 'illness' or any specific 'disorder' as such. What can definitely be said of psychopaths is that they are not only are disinterested in 'right' and 'wrong'; it

actually means nothing to them -they are basically amoral. Someone who is immoral commits crimes or cheats on their partner 'left, right and centre' or whatever they do knowing it's wrong, the do have the ability to be empathetic (understand how someone else would feel on the receiving end of their behaviour) but they do what do regardless. A person who is amoral is incapable of comprehending the difference between right and wrong. They cannot empathise. This makes them both highly dangerous (as they know no boundaries) and virtually untreatable because the lack of basic cognitive (thought processing) ability to ever understand why something is wrong, no matter how many times this is explained. The murder of Anne Maguire being a prime example of psychopathic behaviour.

Being detained under any section means you kept in hospital against your will. Most sections also allow the hospital to give you medication or other forms of treatment, even if you do not want them (section 35, remand for assessment) is one exception. Under normally circumstances your detention will begin on a locked ward, or even in a hospital that is completely secure. Before you can be granted leave from hospital (regardless of whether or not overnight or even longer) a form called Section 17 must first be completed by your Consultant, even if the leave means being accompanied by one or more hospital staff (the form will state how many escorts, if any, are required, which sex and so on) and some Sections (e.g. Sections 37 & 41) require approval by the Secretary of State for Justice before your Consultant can grant the Section 17. Other sections (e.g. Section 35 or 36) cannot have a Section 17 by law, as if detained under either of this you are regarded as being a remand prisoner even though you are in hospital on a Court order. If you are held on one of the emergency sections (i.e: Sections 5(4), 5(2) and Section 4) you could in theory be granted Section 17 leave, in practice, however, this is very unlikely. If you try to leave the ward permanently while detained, or temporarily but contrary to the conditions of your Section 17 (if applicable) the staff can and will make all efforts to stop you. If you succeed in escaping or absconding from hospital (or fail to return from section 17 leave) you will liable to arrest by the police and return to the hospital. Under sections 35, 36, 38, 47 & 49, and 48 & 49, should you escape or abscond or even attempt to, this is serious offence in itself. These sections are explained in more detail in Part Three of this book (Criminally detained patients).

If you are under arrest on suspicion of an offence (and the police realise you have mental condition) you may be sectioned at the police station and then either bailed, or if the charge is not too serious the police may decide to caution you or take no action at all. In any event, at all times your interests will be looked after by an 'appropriate adult' (usually a social worker or psychiatric nurse). It is the responsibility of the appropriate adult to ensure you receive any reasonable support or care you need whilst in police custody.

Also, if you have been taken to a police station as a "place of safety" under section 135 or 136 (this is explained later) you will be assessed by a doctor at the police station and either admitted to hospital (whether under section would depend on your mental health state and if you were willing to be admitted) or the doctor may decide admission to hospital is not necessary.

If you are held on one of the Sections under which you are entitled to apply to the Tribunal from time to time, you will automatically qualify for Legal Aid which will cover 100% of any legal costs if you require a solicitor to represent you (it is well worth engaging solicitor, Tribunals have a very low success rate at the best of times, and trying to represent yourself won't help and as there is no financial benefit in doing so, in my opinion, don't bother). If applying for Manager's Hearing, a solicitor can represent you but you will have pay the full cost yourself. The Tribunal is made up of 3 members; a psychiatrist (doctor who specialises in mental disorder), the Tribunal president who will be a solicitor (or if you held on a restriction order - see chapter 12, or a Transfer from prison - see chapter 13, a judge) and a lay member. The tribunal will examine oral evidence given by you, your nearest relative under the Act, if he or she attends the tribunal, your Consultant, ward nurse and social worker, plus written evidence from your Consultant; and other professionals as well from anyone who agrees to provide you with a 'reference' stating you are well enough to come off section.

Also, prior to Mental Health Review Tribunals you can request any doctor known to you, to carry out an independent assessment of whether you should stay on section, and this assessment is paid for out of public funds. You do not have to submit the independent doctor's report if you think it will harm your case, however if you want a second or subsequent medical assessment you will have to pay the entire cost yourself. On sections 2, 3, 7, 37 or 17a you can also ask your doctor directly to discharge you.

If you are under a hospital based section, or CTO or a voluntary patient considering psychosurgery you have the right to ask have an Independent Mental Health Advocate:

An IMHA is an Independent Mental Health Advocate who especially acts on behalf a hospital inpatient detained under The Mental Act, or a person in the community subject to Community Treatment Order. They were first introduced in 2009 as part of the Mental Health Act 1983 Amendment Act. It is the responsibility of an IMHA

to provide the following services to anyone so detained to enable to patients held under The Act to be aware of, an understand:
- Your rights under The Mental Health Act
- Rights of others, regarding you, while you are under The Mental Health Act
- Parts of The Act which apply to you
- Any applicable conditions or restrictions under the Mental Health Act
- Medication
- Reasons for prescribed treatments
- Safeguards that apply regarding your treatment
- How to appeal

An IMHA can also:
- Help you exercise your rights including speaking up for you and acting on your behalf if necessary
- Assist in decisions about your care
- Gain access to records, with your agreement (if you are considered to lack the capacity to consent to the IMHA accessing your records, the record holder must (a) assume it is in your best interests to have an IMHA and (b) ask the IMHA which parts of your notes he or she wishes to examine and why he or she feels access is appropriate or necessary

An IMHA will:
- Spend time with you, and get to know your opinions on treatment, care and so on
- Visit you in private (if appropriate)
- Support you at meetings, if you wish

An IMHA cannot:
- Act as a substitute family member, friend or carer
- Give legal advice
- Act as a substitute therapist, doctor or nurse

An IMHA will not disclose any information you give them, unless you tell otherwise, unless life is endangered or the information involves criminal activities

Also, on any section, you have the right to complain to the Mental Health Act Commission (this is not the same as the Tribunal, the Commissioners do not have the power to discharge detained patients). The Commission are there to make sure you are cared for properly while detained in hospital, and if they find (or even suspect) you are not, they can something about it.

Chapter 5 – Compulsory detention of informal patients and emergency admission for assessment

Nurses holding power (Section 5(4))

If you are an informal patient (NOT voluntary) and you attempt to discharge yourself or temporarily leave the hospital, when considered a risk to yourself and/ or others, you may be detained by a psychiatric nurse of staff grade or higher for up to 6 hours or until the arrival of a doctor, whichever is the sooner. If this happens, then you will be issued with a leaflet setting out your rights. If you are detained under section 5(4) you cannot be compelled to receive treatment except in an emergency. There is no right of appeal while held under Section 5(4)
If by the time the 6 hours has lapsed, you have not been seen by a doctor or the doctor feels it is not appropriate to extend your detention; you will be free to leave or remain in hospital as a voluntary patient. As such UNLESS THERE IS A SIGNIFICANT CHANGE IN CIRCUMSTANCE you cannot be placed on a section 5(4) again during the same period in hospital. If a doctor sees you within 6 hours of the RMN (registered mental nurse) imposing the section 5(4) he or she may extend detention by a further 72 hours (see Section 5(2) below). Note the 72 hours begins a soon as the Section 5(2) is imposed, it does not begin 6 hours after the imposition of the original Section 5(4)

Doctor's holding power (Section 5(2))

If you are a patient detained by nurse under 5(4) as above, you may be further detained by one psychiatrist or a GP for up to 72 hours (see above) so that you can be seen by a second doctor. This can also happen directly from informal status if leaving the hospital on a temporary or permanent basis if doing so might reasonable place your own safety and/ or that of other in serious danger. In common with Section 5(4) if you are detained under the section cannot be forced to receive treatment except in an emergency. Also, in common with a 5(4) there is no right of appeal. If you are not seen by a second doctor within 72 hours then you may either leave hospital or stay on as a voluntary patient, with same previously stated rights. If you are seen by a second doctor and he or she does not believe you need to be kept in hospital against your will, you will have the option of leaving hospital or staying on as a voluntary patient in any case.

Emergency Admission for Assessment (Section 4)

This power is used to take someone into hospital directly under section, as opposed to detaining patient already admitted on an informal basis (although it does apply for a maximum of 72 hours in the same way as section 5(2)). For obvious reasons, you cannot simply be 'whipped off the street' or 'grabbed' out of your own home and 'bundled' into hospital. As a result, to comply with your human rights, you would have to already be in police custody under the provisions of Sections 135 or 136 (see chapters 7 & 8) or under arrest on suspicion of an offence. If you were under already arrest for an alleged offence when detained, you would either be freed on police bail upon the Section 4 being imposed or cautioned or no further action taken, and thus effectively discharged to the custody of the hospital. In common with sections 5(4) and 5(2), under section 4 the patient is not (except in an emergency) compelled to receive treatment, has no right of appeal, and if the patient is not seen within 72 hours or the section 4 is not converted to a longer section the patient has the right to leave hospital or stay on with full voluntary rights.

Chapter 6 – Admission for assessment (Section 2)

If you are currently detained under doctor's holding power (section 5(2)) or section 4, and a second doctor examines you within the 72 hours, and he or she believes you may have a mental disorder that warrants your detention , you can be held for up to 28 days under section 2 for assessment (and compulsory treatment if deemed necessary). You have the right of appeal to the Mental Health Review Tribunal (a statutory body that makes sure patients are not unlawfully detained). Under the provisions of section 2, if you wish to apply to the Tribunal, you must do so within 14 days of being detained under Section 2 of the Act. If you are detained under section 2, and do apply to the Tribunal for discharge, you will be entitled to free legal representation (regardless of income). You may also apply to the Hospital Managers for discharge (as can your nearest relative) - however if you do and requires legal assistance at a Manager's Hearing, Legal Aid will not be available.

Richard Weaver

Chapter 7 – Admission for Treatment (Section 3)

A patient may be placed on a 'treatment order' (section 3) either if previously subject to a section 5(2) - (see page 16), or section 2 (see page 18). The section lasts initially for up to 6 months, after which the Responsible Clinician (doctor responsible for detained patient) may renew the section 3 for a further 6 months and then in periods of 12 months at a time.

In order to impose a section 3, agreement must be reached between 2 doctors and an 'Approved Mental Health Worker' (usually a social worker), and a diagnosis would need to have been made, all three parties must then agree that it is necessary to detain the person for compulsory treatment, for the safety of the patient, or others. The effects of the compulsory treatment powers mean that if the patient refuses treatment and there is no other viable way to administer, staff have the power under the Act, to administer a forced injection.

In the first 6 months the patient may appeal to the tribunal once (see section 2, page 18) and if he or she withdraws the application may reapply during the same six month period. If the section 3 is renewed after 6 months, the patient may again apply once at any time during the next 6 months (again the patient has the right to withdraw the application and reapply within the same period). After this, the patient may apply once a year while detained under section 3. If a patient wishes to be represented at a Tribunal by a solicitor, the legal aid scheme covers 100% of the patient's legal costs regardless of the patient's financial status. Patients may apply to the Hospital Managers for discharge from section 3 effectively as often as they wish, although should they require legal representation at a Manager's hearing they will be required to find the legal fees from their own funds.

Richard Weaver

Chapter 8 – Removal of patient by police (Sections 135 or 136)

If a police officer witnesses (or receives reports of) any person in a public place who appears to be mentally disordered and the officer has 'reasonable cause' (a somewhat subjective term that really means in his or her opinion) to believe that the person may endanger themselves and/ or others (standard grounds for detention under the Mental Health Act) the officer may detain the person (force is permitted the patient resist). The police have the power to then take the person to either a police station or other "Place of safety" i.e. secure psychiatric facility (usually a special 135 assessment unit) where the detained person can be held for a maximum of 72 hours during which time he or she can be seen by a doctor. If either 72 hours lapse without a medical assessment taking place or a doctor feels it unnecessary to initiate compulsory admission to hospital; the person may be offered voluntary admission, but otherwise would be released from the police station or 135 Unit, and would be free to resume their normal daily activities. On a warrant from a Magistrate, police can exercise much the same powers regarding someone in their own home (including forced entry and even forcible removal from their premises and into custody if necessary). This is called a Section 136. In theory, if the patient resisted police entering their home or being escorted to a police station or other "Place of safety" could be charged with resisting arrest or obstruction or both (depending on what the resistance actually involved). In practice, however, the police would probably regard the resistance displayed as being due to the person's poor understanding of their own behaviour and thus not do so. A person detained by police under a Section 135 or 136, although in legal custody, is not under arrest on suspicion of any offence, so these two sections count as civil sections, rather than criminal ones.

Richard Weaver

Part Three - Mental Health Act 1983 Criminally detained patients
(Note The Insanity Act is not covered in this work)

Chapter 9 - Court remands (Sections 35 or 36)

If you are facing a Court appearance, and a doctor feels you need to be assessed in hospital, to see if there is any direct relation between your offence and your mental disorder, he or she can recommend to the Court you are remanded under Section 35 of the Mental Health Act for a period of assessment. You can be placed on a Section 35 by a Magistrates or Crown Court, but not in conjunction with Magistrates committing a case to the Crown Court. The reason for this is that Section 35 last initially for 4 weeks and can be extended to a maximum total of 12 weeks. Given that when a Magistrates Court commits a case to Crown, there is no actual date set for the hearing, it follows there would no way of knowing if the trial would come up within the maximum of 12 weeks, and in the meantime, what does the Court do with the defendant? However, if already in hospital under section 35 you can be remanded on bail from committal (on or off section) or if remanded in custody from committal, may be made subject to a direct transfer to hospital under sections 48 and 49 (see chapter 14).

After assessment under section 35, if two doctors agree you have a mental health disorder, they will usually recommend to the Court that your offence is dealt with by way of a Treatment (Hospital) Order; assuming your offence is deemed to at least largely due to your illness or disorder If your offence is considered to have little or nothing to do with your condition, a psychiatric probation may be applied for, however if the charge is serious enough that it MUST be tried at a Crown Court, the chances of a prison sentence will be high, especially if you have previous convictions. Offences committed under the influence of drink or drugs cannot be regarded as being acts of diminished responsibility. It may be argued that in some cases you become addicted to drink or drugs as a result of long term depression, and commit a crime under the influence of one or the other, meaning the offence and depressive illness were indirectly linked. Whilst a court could choose to take this into consideration and thus impose a non-custodial sentence, an offence committed under such circumstances STILL could not be dealt with by way a hospital order. If the drink or drug use had caused permanent brain damage (as opposed to a temporary alteration in state of mind while drink/ drug are active) and a crime was subsequently committed, then the making of a hospital order would be a viable option. NB, as will be seen in Chapter 10, a court cannot impose a hospital order without the recommendations of two doctors. Also, with the penalty fixed by law at life imprisonment; a hospital cannot be used as a disposal in a murder conviction, if you were happened to be on trial for murder (hopefully not) the mandatory life sentence is avoided by pleading guilty to manslaughter on the basis of diminished responsibility (genuine lack of full control over your own behaviour owing to effect of mental condition).

Section 36 is remand for treatment, so it follows that unlike Section 35 you can be given medications or treatments regardless of whether you want them or not. In common with Section 35, this section applies initially for 4 weeks and can be renewed for 4 weeks, and then 4 more. Once 12 weeks have expired you can no longer be held on a Section 36. You can only be remanded on Section 36 by a Crown Court. This course of action would normally be taken if you have pleaded not guilty to a charge at Crown and the Court feel it too dangerous to free you on bail prior to your trial, but you are too unwell to be held on remand in prison, you can be remanded under the Section 36 for compulsory treatment.

It must be clearly understood that if you are remanded on a Section 35 or 36, the Court by using the power of the remand is literally using the hospital as a prison (meaning you would have by law to be held on a locked ward). More importantly if you escape from the hospital, or even attempt to; this is an offence in itself, equivalent to escaping (or attempting to escape) from prison, an offence sufficiently serious that it **has** to be dealt with at Crown Court and carries a maximum sentence of 10 years.

Chapter 10 – Hospital Order (Section 37)

If you are convicted of an offence in a Magistrates' or Crown Court, normally punishable by imprisonment (except murder, see Section 35, page 18) a Court may sentence you, upon recommendation by two doctors to indefinite detention and treatment under Section 37. The term 'indefinite' is a little misleading; the responsible consultant can discharge a Section 37 at any time (unlike Sections 37 & 41 where only the Tribunal can discharge) and while in force much control over the section is in the hands of the Ministry of Justice, rather than the consultant. Section 37 operates in much the same way as section 3, i.e. it applies for 6 months, renewable for 6 months and then in periods of 1 year at time. Like Section 3 you can be given treatment or medication even if you do not want it. The main difference between Section 3 and Section 37 as that on Section 37 you will have no right of appeal to the Tribunal in the first 6 months (If the section is renewed after 6 months you can then apply once for a Tribunal at any time during the second 6 month period; and thereafter once per year throughout the time you are kept in hospital. Manager's Hearings can be applied for as and when desired (same as section 3) and of course as in this instance the section is effectively a sentence, you have the right to appeal to the Court against being held in hospital. If you wish do this I would recommend you speak to member of hospital staff (and the solicitor or barrister who defended you in Court) as soon as possible.

Richard Weaver

Chapter 11 Interim Hospital Order (Section 38)

A Crown Court can make an interim Hospital Order, if you are convicted of an imprisonable offence (except murder) prior to passing sentence if recommended by 2 doctors, including 1 doctor from the receiving hospital. In common with a full Hospital Order (Section 37) you may be given treatment even if you do not want it. However, unlike a Section 37, there are no rights of appeal to the Hospital Managers or Mental health Review Tribunal (you or your barrister can ask the Court to review the Order); and Section 17 leave is not permitted by law under this section.

At first, an Interim Hospital Order may be imposed for a maximum of 12 weeks, renewable in periods up to 28 days at a time (if recommended by the 2 doctors) but may not last more than 52 weeks in total. The Judge may, if he or she sees fit, terminate the Order prior to the expiry of the current period in force and deal with the offence by way of a Hospital Order (with or without restrictions) or you may be given a prison sentence or any other disposal the Judge considers appropriate in the light of psychiatric reports. Likewise, if the Order runs its full course, the Judge can sentence the offence by Hospital Order or any other course of action he or she feels is the best way to dispose of the case.

If, while subject to an Interim Hospital Order; you escape or abscond from the hospital itself or in transit to or from hospital/ court (or even try to) - you will be liable to arrest, return to court and the Order will be terminated. If this happens, you will sentenced as though you had no mental health issues.

Richard Weaver

Chapter 12 – Hospital Order with restrictions (Sections 37 & 41)

If you are convicted in Crown Court of an offence (or committed to Crown by a Magistrates' Court after conviction) where the penalty is not fixed by law (i.e. NOT murder) and the Court considers there would be a serious risk of you reoffending if discharged from hospital, the Court may (with evidence from 2 doctors, of which at least 1 must give oral evidence) impose a Hospital Order (Section 37) and a 'Restriction Order' (Section 41). NB although a Magistrates Court can commit a defendant to Crown for the passing of a 'Restriction Order', it cannot make such an Order itself. As well as the normal compulsory treatment, and detention on a secure ward/ hospital; further restrictions apply, the main ones are as follows:

In order for you to be granted temporary leave from hospital or transfer to another hospital approval has to be given by the Ministry of Justice. To be discharged you will need approval by the Mental Health Review Tribunal (after minimum 6 months in common with a standard section 37). Again, during a brief period, you may appeal to the court against the Restriction Order or even being held in hospital at all.

There are two levels of discharge from Sections 37 & 41: Conditional discharge and absolute discharge. Conditional discharge is almost always granted first, it allows you to live in the community, but you may be required to live at a specific address, continue to receive treatment or attend certain meetings/ groups or appointments. Any breach of such conditions (or if you commit any further offences) you will probably be returned to hospital by the police, and if necessary they will use force.

An absolute discharge, when granted, means you are now free of all restrictions attached the sections you have been detained under, however an absolute discharge is very hard to secure, and if you are absolutely discharged and then reoffend, you face the prospect of a very lengthy time in prison.

Besides such restrictions, your consultant is required to send annual (yearly) reports to the Secretary of State for Justice on progress, behaviour and whatever information the Secretary of State for Justice requires. If you ask the Tribunal to discharge you, the MOJ must be notified, and will submit a report to the Tribunal, based on annual reports from your doctor and the details and circumstances of the original (and any previous) offence or offences.

Richard Weaver

Chapter 13 – Transfer from Prison
(Sections 48 & 49 and 47 & 49)

If you are currently serving a prison sentence and are assessed to be suffering mental disorder to a sufficient degree to need treatment under The Mental Health Act, you can be escorted by prison staff directly to a secure psychiatric hospital or ward, for compulsory treatment (this means you must comply with the treatment). This transfer will be made under the direction of the Ministry of Justice (Section 47). The minimum degree of security necessary would largely depend on the nature of the crime or crimes for which you are in prison (and any previous convictions)

If you are in prison awaiting trial or convicted but have not as yet been sentenced, or you are a civil prisoner, again considered to need admission to hospital owing to your mental health state, the MOJ may direct that you are conveyed (escorted) by officers directly to a secure mental hospital or ward, where, again, you can be given treatment whether you want it or not. This is called Section 48. Unlike section 47, this power of The Mental Health Act can only be used in an emergency. If you are in prison on remand or awaiting sentence for an offence, the nature of the offence - and any offences previously committed - will have a direct bearing on the minimum level of security required for the receiving hospital or ward. If you are civil prisoner, other factors will be taken into account.

In conjunction with either transfer, a restriction directive is imposed (section 49) similar to a Section 41. This requires the hospital to only allow leave as directed by the Secretary of State for Justice, and also means you can be returned to prison once you are well enough.

The main differences between the prison transfers and a Hospital Order with Restrictions are that (1) the patient is not required to wait 6 months before applying for a Tribunal (2) If on a Section 47 and a Tribunal discharge the Order, the MOJ may decide to have you returned to prison to complete your sentence or that you would have been released on parole by then, in which case you are discharged from custody. If on the other hand you are held on a 48 and the Tribunal discharge you, the MOJ are obliged to have you returned to prison. (3) A Section 37/41 is, to all intents and purposes, indeterminate. A Section 47 expires when your sentence does, assuming you are still in hospital then, and in any case counts towards your sentence (if you are serving life imprisonment, a decision regarding release on life licence would be made if a Tribunal discharges you). (4) Time on remand or 'convicted remand' spent in hospital under Section 48 also counts towards any later prison sentence, (although for obvious reasons this does not apply if you are a civil prisoner).

Part Four – Mental Health Act 1983 (Community Sections)

Chapter 14 – Guardianships (Section 7)

Upon discharge from section 3 or 37 (no other sections) you may be received into guardianship upon leaving hospital. This may also happen if you are discharged from informal or voluntary status, or even already living in the community. A guardianship is referred to as a Section 7.

Unlike a hospital based section, although the guardianship can require you to live in a specific place and/ or attend certain activities or appointments, even if you are required to live (for instance) in a care home you cannot normally be prevented from going out (except overnight, then permission will need to be obtained -even then it will be from the home manager NOT your consultant): If you wish to leave the care home unsupported and staff do not think this is wise, unless there is a very good reason, they must trust your judgement. If staff or management feel that leaving the home on a particular occasion is dangerous owing to a short term loss of normal reasoning they can apply to have your liberty temporarily suspended under the Mental Capacity Act. This is completely separate to the Mental Health Act and can be invoked (put into effect) even with a Service user (a resident or patient in a home or psychiatric ward) who is not under the Mental Health Act (you can read more about this in chapter 46). You do not have to receive medications or treatments under section 7 if you do not want to. The times you can apply to the Tribunal are the same as on Section 3 (once in the first 6 months, once in the second 6 months and then yearly for as long as you remain on guardianship). You can also ask social services or your consultant to discharge you directly.

Richard Weaver

Chapter 15 – Community Treatment Order (Section 17a)

A CTO can only be used if you are discharged from section 3 or 37 into the community without being discharged from section in the meantime directly onto the CTO. The Section 17a is fairly similar to a Section 7 Guardianship Order, in that it does not require an official Section 17 Leave of Absence form to filled out by your consultant (as would be required with a hospital based section) and similarly to Section 7, under normal circumstances you cannot be prevented from going out with or without staff, as you choose (it is very unlikely that if you are subject to a Community Treatment Order you would live in their your home, as it does involve greater powers which would be hard to enforce if you did).

Apart from being required to live where directed (and possibly attend certain activities or appointments) as you might on section 7, the provisions (rules) of a Community Treatment Order can also require you to take medications, maybe see a psychologist or attend college, voluntary work or whatever. If you fail to comply, staff are not in a legal position to force you to take your medication or generally comply with the conditions of your CTO, however, in all probability they will notify your consultant who may decide to revoke your CTO, which would mean recall to hospital, and if this happens you will automatically be held on a Section 3. If you are recalled (and therefore re--sectioned) the Hospital Manager's will immediately make an application to the Mental Health Review Tribunal on your behalf.

Richard Weaver

Part Five – Protecting yourself in the Community

Chapter 16 - What is abuse?

Abuse is any person (staff member, fellow resident or patient, visitor, contractor or any member of the public) doing things to you that you do not want. The following are examples:

1. Stealing your money, or possessions or pressurising you into lending or giving them away (including asking to "Borrow" something, say tobacco) with no intentions of actually repaying you.

2. Hitting, kicking or head-butting you etc, or striking you with a weapon (e.g. a pool cue) or causing more serious injury (and possibly death) with an implement such as knife.

3. Shouting or swearing at you, calling you names such as "Stupid" or "Idiot" or criticising you because of your skin colour, hair colour, weight, fitness level, degree of intelligence, disability, whether you are gay, straight, bi-sexual or asexual (not interested in sexual relationships) or chosen lifestyle.

4. Staff forcing you to take medication when you don't want to (if you are in hospital under sections 2, 3, 37, 37 & 41, 47 & 49 or 48/49, this does not apply). As I pointed earlier if you are a Community Treatment Order, staff cannot make you take your medication, but if you are recalled to hospital (and therefore automatically go on Section 3) hospital staff can make you take it.

5. Staff are not allowed to detain you in your room as a punishment .In hospital - if it's absolutely essential, staff can keep you in seclusion (a small secure room on the ward used when your anxiety levels are so high you need to be kept away from other patients). If this is done case, staff must constantly monitor your mood, anxiety levels, and so on and they must also release you from seclusion at the earliest safe opportunity.

6. Staff are not allowed to deprive you of your property as a punishment (although I mentioned in Chapter 1 about the practice of nurses stopping patients from smoking as a punishment, this is in fact illegal). If you are old enough to legally smoke (i.e. 18 or over) unless smoking is completely not allowed where you happen to be at the time (e.g. a police station) to prevent you smoking is, in simple terms, contrary to your human rights. Also, staff are not allowed to stop you doing things you enjoy as a punishment - this includes going out. Staff can only stop you going out if you are

under a section and you are not currently permitted leave under your section (assuming you are on a section where authorised leave is an option) or where you do have leave, your mental health state at the time of wishing to go out makes it temporarily very hard for you to make a sensible decision. If you are informal and can be viably sectioned straight away (that is, doing so is both practical and lawful) you can be detained under emergency holding powers Section 5(4) or 5(2) or if you live in a care home or nursing home, the statutory authority agrees to deprive you of your liberty (for a short a time as possible) under the Mental Capacity Act.

7. Unwanted sexual contact from others is abuse, this means rape itself, being 'groped' or generally caressed when you don't want it (sexual contact from staff is abuse even if you don't object). Sexual abuse also includes another person exposing themselves to you, making suggestive comments or forcibly removing any of your clothes (if staff have to strip search you for your safety or that of others) this is the one exception. Even then the search must be carried out in a private area, with no other Service Users/ patients or visitors etc present and the staff who carry the strip search must be the same sex as you are. A member of staff of the opposite sex is not allowed in the room while the search takes place, even if he or she is looking in completely the opposite direction. Staff cannot under any circumstances intimately search you. If there is any reason why this might need to happen, the police would have to carry the search. Again, if the police strip or intimately search you, the search must be conducted in private and by officers the same sex as you are. Likewise, an officer not of same sex may even be in the same room when the strip or intimate search takes place, regardless of whether or not observing the search.

Abuse is a crime. If someone is abusing you, or you see someone abusing someone else, report it. You may inform the police, a social worker, a nurse or doctor, an advocate (advocates are explained on page 13).

Chapter 17 – Being targeted for being 'Different'

To this day, even though I cope well despite, at times, being plagued by several simultaneous issues (problems that occur all the same time), and live a fairly near-normal life in most respects; I can be walking around town just doing my shopping or whatever and a complete stranger will shout something like "Oi, you ginger twat!" or a group of people may pass me in the street and something strikes them as being 'strange' about me (I'm not sure exactly what they pick up on) but whatever it is, the group erupt in laughter. I'm sure sometimes it is a coincidence, they may see me and something else they find funny at the same time. If I believed that every time people laughed when their and my paths crossed; it would probably mean I was quite paranoid. On the other hand, if you know much about the theory of probability (a branch of mathematics that looks at the likely of various outcomes) you would soon realise the chances of every occurrence of this sort of thing amounting to mere coincidence were close to zero. When people do laugh at me, it is completely undeserved, unkind and unfair. Sometimes, when people treat me this way, I am strongly tempted to teach them some manners by punching them hard in the face; however, just trying telling a judge that the "so-and-so" I've assaulted deserved it. At best the judge will be sympathetic but still take a fairly hard line, after all they cannot be seen to condone 'taking the law in to your hands', and at worst would take the view that my actions were completely disproportionate to the provocation, and basically 'throw the book it me' This being the case I choose to control myself. In any case, I could end up picking on the wrong person and be seriously injured. The fact that the other person would then be the one in Court would be no consolation.

Obviously if someone physically assaults you because of illness or disability etc you are within your rights to reasonable force to defend yourself (the same as if someone attacks you for any other reason) however 'reasonable force' is a very loose term. What you, I, or the average member of the public might regard as reasonable force, is probably well over and above the legal interpretation of the term. What makes things far more complex is 'reasonable force' does not in itself mean the avoidance of excessive force, but using (basically) the minimum force necessary under the circumstances. Unfortunately the law makes no allowance for the fact that under attack you don't have the time to assess an appropriate level of force with which to defend yourself, not to mention the fact that in a heightened state of arousal (both fear and anger) you a hardly going to be thinking straight. This is before you even taken in to account the additional problem that if you have some kind of mental heal issue or disability; your reasoning skills are more than likely to be impaired (reduced) to some extent.

Nevertheless, the law is the law, even if it is ridiculous. Whilst you can't be expected to just stand there while someone 'beats the hell out of you', if you can, try and either ward them off, shout for help, run, or a combination of those things. If you have no choice but to physically fight back, try to confine it to a 'good kick in the shins' or something similar (the private parts may be an effective place to kick or knee your assailant) but again you can easily cross the line of 'reasonable force' as the latter will do more permanent damage; whereas although a hard kick to the shins will cause your assailant considerable pain (and possibly bruising) it will do him or her little if any damage in the long run.

Going back to verbal abuse you could simply answer back, and although obviously this is not an offence (unless you use racist or other discriminating terminology) you risk an ever escalating argument (in other words, the 'slanging match') that goes on in a 'downward spiral' resulting sooner or later in one of you physically assaulting the other when your or their temper ignites, and then the same scenario arises of someone being seriously hurt (or dead) and the other person risking prison.

A better way to deal with verbal abuse would be, at least some of the time, take someone (preferably the same person each time) who can act as a witness, if this happens regularly, especially if the person you take with can verify the verbal abuse is regularly coming from the same people. A complaint can then be made to the police, and with any luck those responsible will face some kind of punishment. The person you ask to come out with you doesn't have to be a care worker or anyone in particular, a friend or relative is fine - as long you ask the same person to go out with you when you do request it.

If those people abusing you realise someone is now coming out with you and therefore 'backing off', ask your friend (or whoever) to 'shadow' you. This means he or she hangs back at discrete distance so the bullies think you're alone; and therefore revert to their normal behaviour. If your friend, relative or whoever has a video camera on their mobile phone ask them to film what is happening (your 'shadow' would have to be careful not to give the game away) - then once your abusers have been caught, with the police having video footage, there would be little prospect of your tormentors avoiding a conviction.

You may wonder why some people target those who display 'signs' of mental health issues in the first place, this is a question I have often asked myself!

One obvious explanation is ignorance. People who target the mentally disordered who fall in to this category are stupid enough to believe that people with a diagnosis choose to be the way they are, as if! If choice came in to it and someone chose to be have extra problems (physical, mental or even both) they really would have issues! Therefore, if anyone is foolish enough to believe a person would make that sort of decision (and therefore blame them for their problems) I think they are the ones who are 'mad', so maybe we should feel sorry for them!

Of course, another common reason people 'pick on' those with psychiatric problems is fear. If nothing else, at least this so-called 'reason' makes some sense. Some fear of mental patients probably derives from bad publicity when serious offenders who are (for example) schizophrenic, and go to Special Hospitals like Broadmoor or Rampton, for mass killings or child sex offences: People read such stories in the newspapers or see them on the news, and because the severity of the crimes this overshadows (in the reader or viewer's mind) the sort of behaviour you'd normally expect from someone with this type of illness (whether a lesser offender, or someone is not an offender).

Another kind of fear some people experience (I've personally had fear myself of this kind with autistic adults or adults with severe mental impairments) is when such a person are in a state of considerable agitation, you have no way of knowing whether or not he or she is going to attack you. Unfortunately, the way some people deal with kind of potential threat is to attack first (the old animal instinct that attack is the best form of defence - what angers me about this approach is that as human beings; especially in the so-called 'enlightened' 21st century, people should know so much better). I'm glad to say, even when people behave in an aggressive manner that frightens me, I have *still* choose not to deal with my fear this way.

Some people choose to bully those with mental health issues simply because they happen to enjoy bullying in general (people inclined that way normally have very low self-esteem, i.e. sense of self-worth). The only way (as far as they're concerned) of dealing with this is to put others down, which makes them look better in comparison. People who enjoy bullying for its own sake find the mentally ill (and especially those with learning difficulties) a 'soft target', as they often don't retaliate even if are they physically capable. Sometimes, though, such bullies get more than bargained for when someone they think is a 'soft target' turns around and gives them such a good hiding, they spend the next few weeks or even months in a general hospital! Although, for the reasons I set out earlier in this chapter, this is highly inadvisable, such action can, at times, be perfectly well understood.

Going back to my earlier comments about being financially abused, I am reminded of something that used to arise from time to time when I was between the ages of 16 and 17. At the time the minimum legal age at which a person could smoke in Great Britain was 16 (unlike now where the law requires a minimum age of 18). Anyway I smoked back then; I was in paid employment, so I had the means to support my addiction. Getting to the point, periodically, when I was walking around town, lads my age would come up to me and demand "Giz a fag!" it never occurred to me to refuse. One day some young man did this, and it just so happened I was in quite a good that day so I not only gave him a cigarette, I even cheerfully added "There you go mate-". But he wasn't finished yet: he then demanded "Giz a quid!" I stared at him open-mouthed for a moment and suddenly my whole demeanour changed from charitable to (frankly) suddenly quite angry (he had pushed his luck too far). So I snapped "Fuck off, I'm not giving you a quid!" expecting him to back down. He didn't. Instead he glared and ordered me to "Fuckin' giz a quid!" I remember standing my ground "No!" I said firmly. He called out to his mates (who, thankfully, for some reason didn't respond). Although I was no good at handling confrontations at the time, I felt I had to do something. I violently shoved the guy backwards and told, in no uncertain terms "Get out of my way!" before barging past him and walking home, seething inside. I remember soon after this promising myself no-one was going take advantage of me like this again.

There seems to be another issue here, something seems to alert other people to someone else's, illness/ condition almost as if their mental disorder had some kind of 'magnetism' about it.

However, regardless of whether people fear, judge or simply want to use those with mental disorders or learning difficulties, and why they choose to do so, they have no right to physically, verbally, sexually or financially abuse them. It is (as I said in the previous a chapter) an offence, in fact it is an offence on two counts: (1) abuse of whatever type and (2) contrary to the Disability Discrimination Act.

Chapter 18 – Strangers trying to take advantage of you

Of course this has been addressed in the previous chapter, but now I'm going in to discuss this in more depth. People simply "Taking the piss" in the street are trying to take advantage of you, because they think you won't have the self-confidence to do anything about it. I mentioned in chapter 17 personal experiences of people demanding cigarettes and the final crunch when the young guy pushed it, and then demanded a pound. A few months ago, I went to the local fish and chip shop and two lads (aged somewhere between 9 and 12 years) made the same demand of "Giz a quid!"

My sarcastic response was "Yeah, right" and I walked away. Their response would be better left unsaid - all I will say was it was grossly offensive, they repeated what they were saying over and over; and if they hadn't been children, there is little doubt I would've flattened the pair of them, and I'm sure some men would've done anyway - they probably deserved it but to me, for a grown man to belt a kid - no matter why - is totally off limits. To be honest, by the time I got home I was violently shaking with anger, and could barely talk as I was hyperventilating (breathing excessively fast).

Normally, when people give me hard time the street, it tends to be other guys, the knowledge that half the time I could probably 'deck' them if I chose to, contrary to what you may think, is of little help. Firstly, as I've been at pains to explain earlier, I know it's not worth the bother of arrest (meaning, amongst other things, no smoking while in police custody), a court appearance, a criminal record, probably losing my job plus either a fine or a spell inside. Secondly, although I have the physical ability to be quite viscous, in practice I hate behaving that way. Despite the fact that, at times when I've been very unwell, I have committed a number of quite violent acts - this is not the real me. I actually have quite an acute sense of morality and these days I won't even nick a bar of chocolate, let alone assault a guy unless I'm pushed to the absolute limit.

As result, despite having the physical means to fight back in theory (and I do have the so-called "Gift of the gab"), in practice because my nature is quite gentle I STILL find it almost impossible to deal with. The other point about dealing with bullying or other kinds of abuse by giving the person a 'slap' yourself is that he/ she or they (you won't necessarily be in a 1:1 confrontation) may overpower you and in doing so badly hurt, hospitalise or even kill you. If you happen to be an expert in martial arts, meaning you can still deal with these kind of odds, you then risk multiple GBH or even manslaughter charges if you really seriously 'lose it'.

Between 1993 and1995, I was on rehab ward in a mental hospital in Salisbury. After I'd been there about 6 months, a patient named Gordon (he was in his mid to late 50s) was transferred on to the same ward. Although he was by and large 'all mouth' he'd regularly 'spout off' at people with no provocation (with hind-sight, Gordon should have been in a secure intensive care ward rather a rehab). Anyway, about three times I allowed him to provoke me in to a fight (although as I've already said, I don't normally believe in that sort of thing, I wasn't very well myself and I seriously wanted to 'teach' Gordon to keep his mouth shut). I warned the nurses on a number of occasions that soon Gordon was going to push me way too far...

In December 1995, that's exactly what happened. A slanging match developed into a physical altercation. The fact that I was only 5' 6" and weighed less than 9 stone, and Gordon being 6' 1" and about 11 stone (and ex-army) meant nothing, I was half his age and religiously exercised. I was also in an uncontrolled rage. If staff hadn't intervened I could have been facing a manslaughter or even murder charge – in the event I had my current Probation Order breached (I'd been placed on this nearly 3 years earlier for a pretty inept attempt at robbing a service station). The breach resulted in small fine. It might have been a pain, but was a hell of lot better than outcome if Gordon hadn't survived (plus it saved me being driven insane by the guilt of knowingly killing someone). Whichever way you look at it, taking the law in to your own hands is very dangerous game...

Chapter 19 - "Fair - weather friends"

As well as people bullying "soft targets" for money, cigarettes or favours; there are others who are not so obvious -but still 'false friends'. These are "Fair-weather" or "Candy" friends.

Such people repeatedly 'borrow' money, cigarettes etc; but never repay you, and frankly never intend to. Often they'll make excuses such as "oh I would have done, but money didn't go in the bank" or "Yeah, sorry about that such--and-such cropped up". Of course if you want to borrow off them that's another matter - they'll tell you 'where to go'; or if they do lend, they will charge you extortionate interest rates. My first girlfriend was a good case in point (I'll call her 'Lisa')

I met 'Lisa' in hospital when I was 18, I just been admitted to the secure wing of The Old Manor Hospital (this was the place in Salisbury I mentioned in chapter 18) and (as it happened) I was admitted on a Section 35 (see chapter 9). Anyway 'Lisa' was another patient on the ward, and I actually knew her already (although we were only acquaintances) - so on my first night, I noticed her having a smoke, and asked if her if she had a spare one and she said "I can't lend you one". I remember sarcastically saying "Thanks" and the dirty look she gave me. Luckily, another patient went to the shop for me and picked up some tobacco with some of the money I'd brought in from prison. Of course, when she had no fags she'd pester non-stop, It's a miracle I never completely 'lost it' with her.

Once 'Lisa' (goodness knows how she did it) managed to charm me to be her boyfriend that was it. Not only did she have the immunity of being female preventing me ever physically striking her, regardless of provocation, she was now able to emotionally blackmail me - if I wasn't going to give her something she wanted (usually cigarettes) it was always: "If you loved me, you'd give me one ... "

Heaven knows how I put up with her. As if 2 years of that weren't enough, every few days she'd decide to go out with (and often bed) another bloke, and a few days after that come running back to me begging for another chance! Not only have I had a long running problem with some people of both sexes taking advantage of my good nature, I also suffer from a problem that I'm sure many men do (even those without Asperger's, schizophrenia or any other mental health problem) inasmuch as I find very hard indeed to say 'no' to a woman!

When I was admitted to the ward where I 'Lisa' was being held, there was another patient named Trevor Allen (this really was his name). For a couple of days, he was constantly asking me for smokes, but as soon as his money came through, he made it good, and to his credit, once his benefits were sorted out, because he received considerably more than I did, in fact regularly subsidised me . Trevor, as I soon found out, had learning difficulties (or at least limited intelligence) however that made no difference to my liking of him. Although I was grateful for the financial support he gave me, in no way did I attempt to pressurise him to do so. I simply don't believe in taking advantage of others - I've been a victim of it enough times myself to know how cruel it is.

Time passed. As the law stood at the time, after a non-stop period of 12 months in hospital patients' benefits were cut right down to a paltry amount (back then it was £10.40 per week). Even then back in 1991, this would only cover about 5 packets of 20 cigarettes a week (equal to about 14 smokes per day) -Trevor got through over 40 a day, plus blew money on pork pies, coke and a lot of other bits and pieces. Now it was his turn to scrounge. And beg, and play the guilt game. If all else failed (with some people) he'd resort to physical violence. The person, who had been the best friend I'd known in a long time, was becoming a nightmare!

Then Trevor developed delusions. He believed he had around 120 relatives in Australia and that he was the most senior police officer in the UK. He even began to believe (despite the amount of crap I took from him and my genuine concern for his rapidly deteriorating mental state) that I 'had it in for him'. One night I just asked if he had a light to which he bluntly replied "No" "What?" I began "I'm not giving you a light" Trevor informed me "What's a matter?" I asked, confused "We're supposed to be friends" His response to that could not have possibly been clearer "Fuck off! Go on, get lost!"

My feelings badly hurt; I went to the office and got a light from a nurse. Trevor entered the office about a minute later. His expression was more hostile than I'd even seen it before -far more. "Richard-" Trevor began "You'd better get out of here, or I'm going to hit you..."

Although I heard the words (I must have done else I wouldn't remember roughly 20 years later) I wasn't really listening. The next thing I knew, Trevor was punching me in the face over and over - he was really going for it. When I mentioned the fight with Gordon (the last one, which resulted in a fine) I said I was 5' 6" in stature and weighed less than 9 stone, my statistics were much the same when this happened. Trevor (who was 10 years older than me) was almost 6' and weighed near as damn it 16 stone. However, I had a few compensating advantages; pound for pound I was far fitter, stronger and faster than he was. I was also better coordinated and with a significantly higher IQ, I also had better tactics. The combined factors tipped the scales in my favour -Trevor actually came off worse. But in a way I was the one who lost. Although Trevor's physical pain far exceeded my own when he surrendered (especially as I gave him an almighty kick in crotch!) the mental pain that someone I'd been friends with for 4 years, close friends at that, despite repeatedly bailing him out of money problems, knowing most of the time he wouldn't even try and pay me back, trying to support him when he became chronically ill (as well reluctantly continuing to support his habit , because I sympathised with his financial situation)) and for him to STILL physically attack me with absolutely no wrong-doing on my part TO THIS DAY upsets me. True, the friendship was repaired and I now understand he probably couldn't help it, and when I learned about 10 years ago Trevor had died, I was genuinely upset, nonetheless, the anger of what happened that night and feelings of utter betrayal will probably never completely fade. Although Trevor didn't get very far physically when he assaulted me, this simply didn't and still doesn't make me feel any better. If he had been able, he probably would have killed me that night (it's the same as if the world's worst marksman fires at a gun at and misses by 20 metres, it doesn't alter the fact that he tried to kill you) - I hate to sound unforgiving but part of me doesn't really care whether he could help it or not.

Another good case in point was the Assistant Manager, Marc (not his real name) at the restaurant where I worked as a teenager. This 'Marc' when he first joined the company as a waiter, pretended to my friend, came out with a load of lies about 'his pay being delayed' and borrowing sums of money that accounted for over a week's worth of my wages. He never repaid me, and what's more, never intended to. He also 'befriended' one of the waitresses, just to get her in to bed; and 'ripped her off' for her pains. 'Marc' was also instrumental in arranging the New Year's Eve boxer shorts incident (and by this time he *had been promoted*).

Richard Weaver

Chapter 20 – Sexual exploitation

Men and women with learning difficulties are probably by far the most vulnerable to this kind of exploitation (being taken advantage of). For instance, if a man of normal or above intelligence has consensual sex with a female with learning difficulties who is at least 16 years of age; this is not normally regarded as being a criminal offence. In the same way as the law allows a person 18 or over with learning difficulties to (for instance) smoke, drink alcohol, vote or get married, it views (understandably) that if someone is not to be denied their normal rights as a person over the age of majority (18+) that by the same token (unless it is necessary to section them or otherwise restrict their liberty - for instance Mental Capacity Act) that they have the same responsibilities as everyone else - including being able to say 'no' to sex. But of course saying 'yes' or 'no' isn't just about 'fancying' someone, it encompasses issues around contraception, and a sexual relationship between two people requires commitment, understanding of the need for this and above all involves a huge amount of emotions. I fully accept people with learning difficulties should not be 'penalised' for their disabilities by being denied access to the sort of adult activities that most other people enjoy, but also can see how people of low mental age who try to live totally independently (or very nearly so) can have a lot of addition worries.

For instance, many men dislike using condoms during intercourse. The average woman of at least normal intellect (unless she was planning to have children) would tell the guy "Wear one, or bog off!" It may not occur to a woman of low mental age that she could become pregnant (or catch AIDS, VD etc) by having unprotected sex, so for unscrupulous male who wanted to get away with having unprotected intercourse (and leave the woman to deal with the aftermath) a woman with reduced intelligence, but who was attractive and sexually active would be the prime candidate. If she did fall pregnant, it isn't likely to occur to her to pursue child support claims - he gets off 'scot free' and of course because she consented -she has no comeback. Into the bargain (thankfully not that many of us blokes like that, but - if she's saved up years' worth of social security benefits, he might decide to con her out of that too).

Men with learning difficulties could be just as vulnerable. To put it bluntly, I'm not 'thick' by a long chalk, and certainly a lot brighter than 'Lisa' as I called her earlier -but that didn't stop her 'cleaning me out'. Imagine how a woman with an IQ over 130 could 'use' an adult male with the mental age of a 10 year old to her advantage! While I'm on the subject, being fairly intelligent didn't save me from being coerced in to a homosexual act at the age of 17 (not to mention being conned out of £150 in to the bargain). If the authorities were aware of the details, I could have been sectioned under a Section 3 on the grounds of being unable to guard myself against serious exploitation. It seems terrible indictment that some people (for instance someone with Down's syndrome) and those who have this disability tend be very pleasant, mild mannered and harmless people - have be kept under lock and key to protect them from some of the most unscrupulous people, when it should be those unscrupulous people who are incarcerated (put away).

Chapter 21 – True friends

True friends lend as well as borrow (and they don't charge interest). You do them favour, but they reciprocate (they don't charge 'fees'). A friendship is an alliance, not a business arrangement, let alone a one-sided contract off being 'ripped-off' whenever your 'friend' feels like it.

As well as material support, a friend might (for instance) help you load your van with a load of junk to take to the tip - which you repay him for by having the children when he and his partner go out late; friends work together on 'deeper' levels, the depth of friendship increasing as you get to know, trust and like each other. You might support your friend if his (or her) close relative or partner has died, but equally if your friend really is friend you should be able to confide (and be supported by them) as also you share in one another's joys as well as losses. I am taking this opportunity to offer a word of warning about shouldering too many of your friends' problems:

A few months ago a friend of mine (for reasons of confidentiality I won't reveal the name) had become increasing psychotic (displaying symptoms of mental distress). Unlike the situation with Trevor, there were no issue with one-sided issues of 'take, take, take' but I did have to cope with my friend constantly running away from, being violent towards staff at times, verbally attacking me 'at the drop of a hat' not to mention I was constantly trying to effectively act as a psychologist and a Dad to my friend at the same time as dealing with my own numerous problems. I can gladly tell you, my friend has been well for a few months now, but when my friend was ill and all the turmoil I described above was going on, it almost destroyed our friendship and put me back in a mental hospital. One other thing, sometimes even true friendships disintegrate, and frankly it's not always clear why. A good case in point involves a friend I'd been with from 1999 to 2013. Again, to maintain confidentiality I will not use this woman's real name - I'll call her "Sue".

Without going into a whole load of confidential (and frankly irrelevant) information, "Sue" moved into the same secure unit in 1999 as I had resided for previous 3 years. "Sue" and I had quite a lot in common, we both had Asperger's we, we'd both been the nick for similar offences and we'd both endured physical, financial and yes, sexual abuse (remember there was the guy I mentioned who coerced me in to gay sex). Anyway, "Sue" and I quickly became friends. After she left the unit in 2.004, I kept in weekly telephone contact and in 2009 we ended up in a care home together. I was only there a few months, and then ended in hospital; "Sue" and I regularly wrote to each other. When I was discharged, and moved to my current address, I began visiting "Sue" once a month by rail (no cheap past time) and in January 2012 "Sue" wrote to me and said she no longer wished to be my friend. In the March, the friendship was revived, only for the same thing to happen in July 2013 – Heaven only knows what she was thinking!

Chapter 22 – Agencies who can stop you being abused

I briefly mentioned the Mental Health Commission in chapter 4, there is one other main organisation that specialises in looking after those in care, this agency is known as The Care Quality Commission (formerly CSCI) who inspector psychiatric and general hospitals, plus care homes and nursing homes countrywide. Also, charities such as MIND can point you in right direction. Samaritans will offer a listening ear, and be supportive but it is against their policy to advise or provide practical assistance.

Often, I'm sorry to say, when abuse involves staff abusing patients or residents, the police are rarely interested especially if the complainant happens to be on a section. I remember early in 1991 watching a TV programme about Rampton Special Hospital. On one of the female wards, several of the patient complained they'd been raped by male nurses (and there was evidence of semen on the bed sheets). Even if the patients in question had consented, with the combination of being sectioned (and therefore regarded as vulnerable) and the fact that then nurses in question were in a position of power, as far as the law would be concerned - it would be rape, full stop. The police did attend the hospital and spoke to the complainants for about 5 -10 minutes, before having drinks, and a 3 hour laugh and joke with the nurses about the allegations. After this the police coerced the women to sign a form agreeing to drop the allegations.

A social worker will always be a good person to liaise with, if there are problems (I know in some high profile cases e.g. the Baby P scandal, Social Services in those situations have proved to be useless; fortunately there are many good ones). I've always believed that in area of life, a 'few rotten apples' stand out so glaringly it creates a totally false impression of being the norm -in actual fact, the opposite is probably going to be case.

Advocates (which I'll cover later) are people who visit patients in psychiatric hospitals held under The Mental Health Act. They don't powers like the Mental Health Commission or The Care Quality Commission, but they will speak for up you (putting things across from your point of view).

You could, if the problem is serious, hire a solicitor and pursue a civil prosecution (where if you 'win' the defendant will probably be ordered to pay compensation, and if you lose you must pay legal costs) or even a private criminal prosecution (this where the offender is still tried in a criminal court) but the prosecution process does not go through the police. If you want to go down this route, <u>unless know can comfortably afford legal fees, check your situation regarding legal aid</u> as it may not be automatic.

Richard Weaver

Part Six - Self help

Chapter 23 – Nobody can do it for you

Whilst there are various agencies who can support you in various ways e.g. DWP and funding authorities deal with financial support, doctors and nurses diagnose and treat, between them, family and friends can visit, offer emotional support (and professionals including psychologists and social workers can also provide such support) there is one key player without whom you will never get it together. That central person is YOU. If you don't believe anything is amiss in the first place, or won't be helped or even accept help but refuse to 'own' part of the process (the attitude that "You're the doctor, you sort it out, and that's what you get paid for"). I'm sorry but such approaches are complete non-starters. I'll give a few examples:

When at the Hayes Unit (where I met "Sue") there was male resident who, again for reasons of confidentiality, I will withhold his name and call him "X". This guy would shout, scream and bang walls almost night without fail. He'd also quite happily run around naked regardless of whether or not there happened to be female staff or Service Users in the vicinity. He would also swear or start shouting at people, but the worse thing was that most time he saw nothing wrong in his own behaviour. I am convinced that does not mean "X" is a psychopath. In his lucid moments (which were pretty few and between) he did understand. Nevertheless he saw no reason to even try and control himself or seek out staff support. Admittedly, he would sometimes tell staff when was hearing voices, but that was about it. This dragged on for a few years and "X' would wonder why he remained on section.

We've had residents where I am now who saw nothing wrong with their own behaviour. One particular guy stole food (and a whole packet of my tobacco on one occasion), swore (without good reason) and tried to bully young female staff members. He also displayed a lot other anti-social behaviours. One female member of staff who always keen to help anyone out, often bore the brunt of his abuse during the very times she was bending over backwards to help him (one day he was abusing Tess when she was trying to help him, and quite frankly, I lost it and floored him - but that's another story). The point is this guy was fooled by a common misconception you take your medication, do your bits a pieces, a few months pass and then, bang you're better! Unfortunately it doesn't work like that.

Going back to the place where "Sue" and "X" lived, another male resident (I'll call him "A") used to go in to other residents rooms and steal money, masturbate in the lounge (and from his point of view, if a female staff member or service user caught him - then so much the better). He also (while she and I were still friends) tried to go for "Sue" who stands at little over 5' (compared to this guy's 5' 11") and she weighed well under 8 stone against his 15+. As well as the fact "Sue" was my friend at the time, I hate bullies (especially men who bully women) consequently I stepped in way, grabbed this guy's arm and warned (truthfully) if he did it again I'd cripple him. In case you're wondering why I side-track from time to time (especially in the area of challenging behaviour, and getting in to the realms of me wading in, and the detail) let me explain. It's not that I've got an ego problem and therefore need to compensate by boasting about how 'good' a fighter I am, it's just that when these incidents have arisen I have at the time experienced very heighted emotions (I'm considerably calmer these days) hence violence, and as for the degree of detail, it puts some person interest in the subject matter, and to be fair it enables my readers to 'know' me better, and I need to go into more detail when referring to specific events for clarity.

The fourth and final example I'm going to give of someone who in the past hasn't helped themselves is me:

When I first started compulsive absconding from home, when I was 16, I would say (truthfully enough) that I felt someone else was taking control and I was acting against my own will. That was one thing. The trouble was the next time the 'urge' to run away came over me I would neither tell anyone, nor would I fight the compulsion. As my behaviours got worse, starting with dodging train fares, through shop-lifting and bilking restaurants (ordering meals with means or intention to pay) I moved on to credit card fraud before that fateful day (1st October 1990 - I'll never forget it) when travelled from Winchester to Southampton and attempted to rob a building society with a toy gun. Take the attempted robbery itself as a good example: I'd actually 'discussed' the crime with my 'voices' the night before. If I'd used my brains, and done something; anything to raise the alarm; instead of wading in to a crime that I still regret, cost me time in prison, and later time on a Hospital Order; gained me a criminal record, and put two cashiers through what must have a terrifying ordeal, after all they had no way of knowing the gun wasn't real, which was the idea at the time. The only good that came out of this crass and frankly serious crime was that the authorities finally saw to it I received help, and being on a section obviously I had to accept treatment. Then began the long, slow journey, of learning to help others to help me. This process only started when I realised I was just going to keep on doing things, being locked up, reoffending upon release and so on (in other words I was a recidivist). At first, the process was very hit and miss (in fact far fewer hits than misses) but once I realised I could help myself, this knowledge encouraged me to increase the tempo and my confidence increased. I have many times been a bit TOO confidant, resulting in what I call a 'blow-out' (a self-harming incident or suicide attempt, running off or even another crime including a feeble attempt at robbing somewhere and a few occasions, arson). On the positive side; it may be a cliché but we all learn by our mistakes. When, as people we get things right, fine, and this encourage us; but when get things wrong, we don't like that one bit, so next time around we try a lot harder (apart of course from those who aren't interested in changing or won't help themselves).

Richard Weaver

Chapter 24 – You can't do it alone either

This was the mistake I made when being over-confident. This happened in two ways: (1) the first example was by far the more dangerous. After I'd been placed on the Hospital Order at Southampton Crown Court, for the robbery charge, I by and large controlled things using my own power, and this worked for long enough that I was able to be discharged from section. This was January 1992. I had a few minor 'wobbles' over the next few months (most it involved running away) and there was also a far more serious issue of taking a massive overdose in the July. In September that year, I finally received my diagnosis of Asperger's syndrome. Whether a coincidence or not, 3 days Trevor (the friend I mentioned who attacked me in the office a few years later) took a taxi to the M3 Services, at Fleet, and I committed my second (rather inept as a psychiatrist later put it) attempted robbery. After a period detained under Section 3, I appeared at Winchester Crown Court and received 3 years' probation with conditions of residing at Gloucester Group Homes, a company providing residential care to adults with autism and Asperger's syndrome (you may recall, I briefly mentioned the incident itself on page 38). Without 'banging-on' too much, the placement broke down in months (large owing to the open door policy and my need at the time of a locked door). Despite the fact that I felt I was on the border of Asperger's and 'normal'; and, regardless of the fact that I believed I did not a locked door, the reality was that I did.

Anyway, I was readmitted to hospital and regularly got myself in 'fixes'; running away and getting stranded, occasional fights, I regularly smashed up furniture with my fist to 'prove' to myself I was 'hard' (back then I did have an ego issue). True, I didn't enjoy fighting, as I've already said I don't particular like violence - so it's important to realise I am not contradicting myself - the fights I did get in, even back then, only arose if the other person 'wound me up to pulp' as with the fights with Gordon, the one with Trevor, of course was purely self-defence.

Having given the background (sorry to be so long winded) my behaviour led to my parents seeking out a secure unit that could treat my Asperger's and my other illness. They found The Hayes. I was so sure I wouldn't need to go there, and I would learn to cope. In fairness if my delinquent behaviour had dragged on much longer I would have ended up in Broadmoor/ Rampton or a Category A prison.

The other, less serious problem being over-confident caused me, is on various isolated occasion exercising my right (once off section) to go out unsupported even when the voices were giving me hell, and taking the view that <u>failure is not an option</u>. Ninety-nine plus per cent of the time that's OK, but setting aside, for a moment, the extra burden my Asperger's syndrome and superimposed illnesses place on me, part of being human is to fail from time to time. Now bring the additional problems back in to the equation, and it becomes clear there are times a person has to swallow his pride and if it's necessary to go out at the same as that sort of thing going on - use the resource of staff (after all, this is what the Service User's funding authorities pay for).

Supported or unsupported leave is barely the tip of the iceberg. You may be in a situation where you feel like self-harming on-site, so the issue of leave may not be the key issue. Of course, if it's a question of leaving the ward or home to buy something to harm yourself with, going out alone-to be perfectly blunt -would be highly risky. If, on the other hand, implements or chemicals that could use for this purpose are already on site, this becomes less straight forward. Don't get me wrong, I'm not saying in any way that if such implements or chemicals are already in the home or on the ward that this makes unsupported leave viable or even any safer, on the contrary if you are determined enough at the time to not need to go out in order to achieve your intentions, it wouldn't be safe for you to go out even with staff. I am not trying to be insulting or patronising by saying this, but if you did go out even with two or three staff supervising and you managed to abscond (remember in such a heightened emotional state you will be full of adrenaline and as such physically capable of far more than you normally would) you would then be in serious danger of severe self injury or death. What does need to happen in this situation is you need to be honest with staff and tell them you feel wretched and want to self harm or even take your own life. Staff can then spend extra time with you, not just to keep an eye on your safety (although this is important) but also to work through the issues that are making you feel so miserable. It may simply be a matter of a couple of days 'one to one' I know myself this can (for just a few days, before it 'gets in your face') be reassuring and calming. I don't believe in people being on one to one for weeks let alone months on end, it soon becomes far too punitive.

Chapter 25 – Resources available

I mentioned being honest with staff. It has already been mentioned that no one can do it for you, nor can you do it alone: this is whole point - your 'recovery journey' is one of collaboration, a partnership, you and your care team (plus friends and family) working as a team. If you choose to deliberately do something stupid then nothing (short of locking you up) is going to stop you.

I know this, because I used to carry out premeditated reckless acts from time to time. True, even if I had not been determined to carry them out, suppose the reverse were true and I was determined NOT to carry them out, I would STILL (at times) fail without support. At the outset, the degree of staff input will need to be high. As you regain your independence the necessary degree will fall as you gradually take the burden of responsibility from staff on to your own shoulders.

Although the work has since dried up, I did some work for the Choice Care Group, helping a member of management train groups of staff in STAR training. Through this work I have learned the 5 stages of progress from 'stuck' (high dependency on staff) to independence. I don't entire go along with the model used, but the principal is correct:

5) No more need of mental health services. He or she is getting on with their own life, but knows how to get help if they become unwell again.
4) Mostly independent. Success spurs person on. Good idea to occasionally monitor person's progress to avoid a catastrophic major set-back.
3) Realise they have to do their share of the work. Aware change is difficult, still prepared to face it. Now knows nothing will change unless they make it.
2) Accept things are very bad. Seeks help and accepts help offered. Relies on others, blames them if things go wrong. Needs to be responsible for errors.
1) Stuck. In denial (maybe even fooling self). Feelings of hopelessness. With luck person will at least realise things may change.

NB You will not progress at a constant rate. Sometimes, you will achieve uniform progress, other times you will plateau, and at others you will regress (go backwards).

Specific resources

Psychology

This has already been briefly touched upon. Psychologists are able to help you develop new ways of controlling impulses or 'temptations' e.g. a voice in your head telling you to "Smash that window". These methods of control are referred to as coping strategies. They can also help you to reinforce existing ones.

If you have, for example, Anorexia (so-called 'slimmer's disease) one way in which psychologists may help you with this is the use of a reward system. You and your psychologist may agree that if you can gain 2 kilos in a month, staff would reward you by taking you to see a rock concert, and the hospital or home would pay for admission and transport (if rock music happened to be your thing).

I have a long-standing problem with what I call 'excess baggage', a problem most people have to some extent. What I mean by the term is memories of quite traumatic events during childhood, adolescence and early adulthood (a beating in the middle of the night at boarding school when was 11 years old, at the hands of half-a-dozen 5th years would be as good an example as any). This particular event took place in December 1983, that's almost 31 years ago but I have never had the chance to draw closure - the saying that time is a great healer, in my opinion is nonsense! Psychologists can help draw closure on unresolved issues.

Occupational therapy

This can include Art Therapy, Drama Therapy or Music Therapy (note this list is by no means exhaustive). It is not important whether or not you are 'good' (or think you are 'good') at these activities or not -remember you are not at college, this is your treatment and it's about what you get out of it.

I am not at all good at art, but this hasn't prevented gaining 'therapeutic value' (to coin a phrase) by having one to one with the Art Therapist, talking to her as I was drawing, the conversations could cover pet subjects of mine for instance maths, railways or law. Other times we would have the kind of day to day 'chit-chat' people have with friends or family. On other occasions the conversations were far more in depth and were like a combined art and talking therapy session. Sometimes, however, I'd choose to sing during our sessions. When it came to Drama Therapy, things were different, firstly -this needed to take place as a group session (drama can be done on a limited one to one basis e.g. role plays -

I'll get back to this point shortly) but for acting out plays it stands to reason several actors or actresses are needed ...

...One of the first Drama Therapy sessions I ever did was one to one, but with a big difference. I played the role of a shop manager interviewing different candidates one at time for a position as a Sales Assistant. The interviewees were played successively by each of the other members of the group. Role play just so happens to be one of favourite types of drama (along with acting out my favourite film quotes to anyone who cares to listen) and as there were no pre-set questions (I had no time to prepare questions either) it was a plain and simple question of improvising. I took considerable trouble not to ask any two 'interviewees' the same questions (six sets of questions to form six interviews each 5 minutes in duration took a lot of ingenuity (but then I like being stretched) and in this one session alone, rising to the challenge of handling something I'd never before even had to plan, let alone 'pull-off' and getting it right first time, was a major tonic. At the end of day this is the purpose of occupational therapy, not just for entertainment (undeniably this is an integral part) but to promote contentment, confidence and other positive emotions. I'm now going to skip the subject of Music Therapy - I think the reader should have got the point.

Industrial Therapy

I briefly mentioned Industrial Therapy quite early on in this work. For patients who are very limited in their abilities, this would consist of rather dull and repetitive work such as packing a certain number of rolls of sellotaped in a package basically for the duration of the working day. Typically, this would be something like 9.30am until 12noon and then 1pm until 4.30pm, Monday to Friday.

Patients of higher capability might carry out engraving or various jobs on a computer. The idea, of course; as part of patients' rehabilitation, is to help them prepare for employment. It's a sad truth that many long-term patients in psychiatric hospitals will probably never compete on the jobs market.

Own resources

A good example of this is turning negative it to a positive. This may sound like a bit of a 'pat answer' but there is some genuine mileage in it. Let me again draw on a few of my own experiences:

1. Asperger's syndrome is referred to by some people as a 'disability' -in some respects having Asperger's is actually quite an

advantage. In common with OCD, people with Asperger's have a high tendency to perfectionism. The 'condition' if we are to call it that; normally encompasses at least average levels of intelligence, and some people with Asperger's are geniuses.

2. Despite voices and the like having their 'down' side, they can also be good company, helpful advisors (especially with a bit of constructive criticism where necessary), and brilliant for bouncing ideas around on subjects ranging from religion to music or sport, to science or films, law, history, you name it. Sometimes they even make up jokes.

3. Another advantage of having Asperger's is the ability to completely focus on something. Quite often, if I'm working on the computer or busy upstairs cleaning and one of house-mates tries to call me, I don't hear them. It's not that I'm 'deaf as a post' although my hearing isn't brilliant, and it certainly isn't the fact I'm deliberately ignoring them - it's just that when I am really immersed in a job, I simply 'switch off'.

4. Logic is yet another useful skill people like myself tend naturally to have an abundance of. Probably why I enjoy maths, it's about as logical a subject can be. For the same reason, chess is a very suitable game for people like me, who have Asperger's.

5. My mood disorder (which happens to be a bi-polar, or manic depression) undeniably is a real pain when I'm down in a dip, but if I get a 'good' high (there are highs and lows) I love it!

6. Mental disorders in general give people affected by them (a more positive perception than people who suffer from them) the edge when working with others in a similar situation. Sure professionals can study, learn on the job and be sympathetic to their clients' needs. The one thing they cannot do is to know first-hand what it is actually like. People who do have whatever form of mental disorder do know first-hand. Being in such a position myself, I know what other people are going through - I've been there myself. I have personal experience as opposed to professional - sometimes this means my friends trust me more than they trust the staff.

Chapter 26 – Crisis teams

Sometimes, when people have been known to the psychiatric services for a while and periodically have (or at serious risk of having) a 'meltdown', they are given a phone number for the local crisis team. If the person recognises the signs of such a breakdown coming on, and for whatever reason it is impractical (or they may not want to) talk to staff, friends or family; they can speak to a member of the crisis team, who are available 24/7. One big disadvantage of this method of coping is that you will not know any members of the crisis team very well, and you rarely speak to the same person. Another disadvantage, although a lesser one, is that when speaking to a member of the crisis team on the telephone - the crisis worker cannot give the same kind of practical help he or she could if there in person. Of course, the same is true of speaking to family members or friends on the phone, but at least they know you, and obviously your family and friends don't change. At any rate what the crisis team member can do is to assess your specific issues and any relevant triggers, and try to work out the next step. I can remember a few times speaking to a crisis worker by telephone, we briefly talked about the causes of my anxiety, the worker and I between us decided that (at a push) I would be able to cope for a few days; meanwhile an emergency appointment was made with my psychiatrist.

There are, by the way, some circumstances when you may see a crisis worker face to face. If it gets this far, the likelihood is you're getting very close to a hospital admission. This last sentence is not intended as a threat. I'm just saying that if one of the crisis need to visit you at home (or a team member visits you in a general ward after attempted suicide) you will displaying all the signs of becoming very unwell and that being the case, your entire care team will be worried about you.

Richard Weaver

Chapter 27 – Using your condition against itself

This technique is something I personally discovered as part of my own self-help policy. I cannot for the life of me remember how I figured out the system I am about to describe, but I can tell you it frequently works for me:

Background

As well as more 'conventional' voices, I experience about four 'entities' (the two that are particularly relevant here are known as "Bridge" and "Galaxy" who are 'good entities' and 'bad entities' respectively). They don't so much talk to me in my head as quite literally through me. Imagine you're an actor or: actress, in a play and there are (say) 10 characters in the play. The difference is, unlike in an ordinary play, you say the lines of all 10 characters. This how the two of them, plus the less prevalent ones, communicate with me - and of course I communicate back, out loud, when 'playing me'.

As I've already briefly mentioned, in the past acting on the advice of 'bad' voices and 'bad' entities has got me in to a lot of problems. Even when I'd reached the point in my life when I almost NEVER acted on the bad advice, at times the subject content (and the intensity) could be so horrendous, it would result in stress levels 'through the roof', the knock-on effect being a self-harm incident or even suicide attempt on my part.

The way of using "My condition against itself" is two-fold. For years I had used "Bridge" to tell "Galaxy" to knock it off (not quite so politely) when being a jerk. However, the method I recently discovered (and I regularly point this out to trainees when I am giving talks about autism) is cause Galaxy to 'shoot himself in the foot'. So consider: one day Galaxy says to me "Go beat the hell out of so-and-so". Instead of (like in the past) getting drawn in to a lengthy, stressful row; I might go and the computer and work on a project similar to this one. I will then 'employ' Galaxy to advise me on typing errors, grammar and so on (owing the fact Galaxy's negative dialogue is very minimal percentage-wise in terms of the number of waking hours and minutes in the day, and the other 99.99% actually being a useful partner - I wouldn't go as far as to say friend - I can use him this to get an important job done, make good use of free time which avoids boredom (one of my biggest enemies) distract myself from the disturbing content of the command and I avoid the anxiety (and ensuing dangerous occurrence) potentially caused by an argument. In chapter 25 I spoke of 'making positives out of negatives'. This system does exactly that, using the positive elements of Galaxy during the vast majority of the time when being constructive, using Bridge to help fight him off when being destructive and also when being destructive, turning the situation around and causing him to work with me rather than against. It's a bit like the old saying "Using the Devil to do God's work"

Chapter 28 – Appropriate use of PRN medication

PRN is an abbreviation in Latin for 'as and when required' (literally it stands for: Pro Rota Nata). I used to sometimes crack a joke that it stands for "Pills required now!"

Joking aside, if you were being bombarded by negative auditory hallucinations (voices) understandably you are probably going feel like 'flipping out': Requesting PRN medication in this sort of situation can be very useful. In chapter 3 I mentioned Chlorpromazine (otherwise known as Largactil) - which you may recall was the first psychiatric drug invented. It might be the oldest anti-psychotic but, certainly in my experience -and I know some friends of who have mental health issues agree -as a PRN medication it is both fast acting (especially in liquid form, and it tastes quite nice in liquid too) and just as importantly it has a powerful sedating (calming) effect. Lorazepam is a newer drug than Chlorpromazine (although it's older than many); it also has a fast acting, strongly sedating effect. The biggest problem with this drug by far is its addictive quality. This being case it should use to the bare minimum.

No PRN drug should be used 'willy-nilly', for two reasons: (1) it can soon become a habit to pop a pill every time you have raised levels of anxiety, rather than using other coping skills and (if possible) tackling the cause rather than symptoms and (2) although medication is designed to fulfil a very important function, obviously the chemicals found in the various drugs are not naturally produced by the human body, so it follows that these chemicals are 'foreign' (which by the way the explains why medications for the treatment of most things physical or psychiatric cause side-effects). This being the case excessive use (which will develop if you come to psychologically or habitually rely on PRN) combined with the drugs you are prescribed for regular use are more or less bound to damage your body. This arising as an unavoidable consequence of using your medication correctly and with beneficial effect is one thing, unnecessary damage due to disproportionately high use of PRN is quite something else. Note - something that is disproportionate is either too high or too low relative to something else - for example wages of £14 per hour being disproportionately high for unskilled labour.

Richard Weaver

Chapter 29 – Keeping busy

I said earlier, boredom was one of my biggest enemies, and I was not exaggerating by any stretch of the imagination. To quote yet another cliché, "The Devil finds work for idle hands". How true this is! Think how many young people when they get involved in petty crime use the excuse "I was bored". Although being bored is no reason (or even decent excuse) for getting up to mischief or in to trouble with the police, if these young men and women actually had something constructive to do (preferably something that stimulated them) they could pour their energies in to those past-times, rather than anti-social ones. Again, have you ever wondered why some people who are unemployed (and therefore on a low income) don't feel the need to steal while others in well paid work do steal? A likely answer is those without jobs who don't steal probably don't want to as it doesn't fit in with their sense of right and wrong, as a result, in order to cope financially they are very careful, and find other constructive things to do during the day (e.g. attending college, to improve job prospects). One reason people in well paid employment may choose to steal anyway (I'm only suggesting a theory) is that their work although rewarding in monetary terms, gives them no job satisfaction, so the risk associated with committing a crime (and the excitement that always comes with risk) may create a welcome diversion from an otherwise mundane routine.

If your life consists of a combination of not being employed or only working a few hours per week, a low boredom threshold, your 'mates' egging you on to 'be Jack the lad', poor self-esteem (you'll recall from early on I explained this means you basically don't like your own image) and the additional burdens mental health problems place on you, the temptation for a little excitement must at times be unbearable.

So, how to keep busy: I'm only in paid employment a few hours each month but I sure don't get bored, on the contrary I'm forever finding there simply aren't enough hours in the day to accomplish all the things on my mental 'to do list'. So, I do the work when it needs doing (about 6 hours per month plus a few hours travelling to and from work). So what else? Well since I started writing this book nearly 3 weeks ago, I have been really absorbed in it. I also spend a lot of time up in my room keeping it pristine clean (I find cleaning my room or the staff room at Sue Ryder when I used to have voluntary job there and cleaning in general very rewarding). By my own efforts I can turn a load of dirt, grime and mess in to order and cleanliness. I spent quite a lot time keeping myself clean respectable looking. It is well worth noting that tasks involving personal hygiene and cleanliness (or jobs that involve cleaning and tidying in general) by virtue of the way they transform chaos in to order, structure and freshness, have an uplifting effect whe11 undertaking them that's in truth quite therapeutic ('peps' you up).

I also do my laundry 3 - 4 times per week, go to the shops most days for tobacco, soft drinks etc, I go food shopping once every week, cook my own food, wash up afterwards, read the papers, go out the train from time to time, the pub - I could on forever.

I may not be 'loaded' (although I'm not 'short' either) but I do find my life satisfying (far more so than when I was in the game of being 'hard' back in old days. True, at the time I commanded esteem from my peers, but external esteem means nothing if inside you feel a 'nobody').

Part Seven – Employment with a diagnosis

Chapter 30 – Voluntary work

Outline

I mentioned in chapter 29 about when worked for Sue Ryder. I did one spell from March 2013 - July 2013, and again from April 2014 - June 2014. I took the job on for a number of reasons, namely: a chance to give something back in return for DWP benefits, the cost to the taxpayer for my accommodation fees in my present care home and previous placements; and restitution for previous crimes I'd committed, both financially, and on a practical level. In addition it was a constructive use of time, a chance to make friends, gain experience in the workplace, and a source of a reference if needed in the future if I applied for paid work.

A lot of the time, I was behind the scenes doing all the 'menial' cleaning jobs, but as I've made perfectly clear, I like cleaning, infact I enjoy working in general, so this did not faze me! Sometimes I was given tasks that were more challenging, stacking books on the shelf in categories (and within each category, by surname of author), on one occasion I was asked to assemble a 'stepper' (a piece of exercise equipment) and I had no instructions. It was a good job, with my previous long-standing gym career that I knew what a stepper should like, fully assembled. Even so, it was a bit of a 'Krypton factor' task, but that was OK too, after all, I always have enjoyed a challenge. I never had a problem with anything management asked me to do. I've had voluntary jobs with other charities in the past, and been assigned work in different shop involving steaming clothes (a very fast alternative to ironing them), vacuuming, using the till and bagging rejects to sell to the rag man. On one occasion I went out in the van helping with inter--branch stock rotation.

A potential employer (in the paid sector) will be impressed by an applicant who is prepared to work for free, and still to a good enough standard for the former voluntary employer to give a good reference. I know if I was an employer looking to hire paid staff, and someone applying for the job had worked for nothing but still had been a good time-keeper, hard-working, clean, well presented, polite to customers and other staff and management, willing and so on; the view I would take is that *if this person is that good when working for free, how good would he or she be if they received payment!?*

Other kinds of voluntary work

There are many forms of volunteering other than shop work. Examples include Special Constables, voluntary medical staff (e.g. doctors and nurses currently treating Ebola victims in West Africa), Samaritans, fundraising for numerous charities, and volunteering for the Council (e.g. litter picking).
So let's have a look thee in more detail:

Special Constables

Special Constables (often known as PCSOs) are basically unpaid police constables, but they carry out the same duties (and have the same powers) as their paid counterparts-of course PCSOs are only part-time. They either have other paid jobs or are seeking work. You may wonder why someone would do the same workload, the same degree of danger, the same unsociable hours and face the same levels of abuse as paid police constables, but without getting paid for it ... well here are two probable explanations: either the particular PCSO is happily employed in work of a completely different nature, but wants to 'do their bit' and make a difference or may currently be out of work/ in full-time education, wants to make a future career in the police force, and in the meantime wants to gain valuable experience, also see if they actually would be happy in this line of employment, and again putting in 'hard graft' when you're not getting paid for it looks good on your CV.

Volunteer medical workers

Qualified doctors and nurses sometimes volunteer to go to places like West Africa to help people severely affected by the Ebola virus. I'm sure that you will know that the work is hazardous, and one 'slip' with measures to maintain workers' safety, could be fatal.
From the point of view of someone using voluntary work as a 'launching-pad' to paid employment, this would only be viable if you have previously worked as a paid and qualified doctor or nurse, and of course held relevant qualifications.
If you do not have nursing qualifications but want to gain some voluntary experience in the caring profession, working as a voluntary care assistant in a hospice could be a possibility.

Samaritans

Samaritans (you may remember) are there to listen and help the caller or drop in client find their own answers to personal issues.

The hours can be unsociable. Samaritans are not allowed to advise, nor are they allowed to counsel. Samaritans owing to the nature of some of the people they work with will sometimes get the brunt of client's frustrations -sometimes they receive obscene phone calls. To be honest, if you've previously had mental problems, unless you have recovered pretty much fully and remained stable for a few years -I'd leave this sort of thing to others. On the other hand, if you genuinely have recovered sufficiently and sustained good mental health long enough to cope with this kind of work - FAIR PLAY!!

Fundraising

All charities clearly need revenue (money) to pay for the services they provide. If we look at Sue Ryder again (but outside of the context of their shops) they generate money in ways other than selling donated and other goods. For instance they may have collections in supermarkets and I happen to know Sue Ryder are currently working in partnership with Morrison's supermarkets in a joint fundraising campaign. It is the job of fundraisers to organise and arrange these kinds of activities or events.

Voluntary work for the Council

A couple of good examples of voluntary work for the Council could be clearing rubbish or gardening. This is fairly easy to get in to as it requires no previous experience. It is also good for people with learning difficulties as most would cope (I spent 3 years on a similar scheme myself, except that we were paid) and even at the level of performance required by a paying employer my fellow workers coped (so did I, for what it's worth, but then I haven't got learning difficulties) so all credit to them.

Richard Weaver

Chapter 31 – Gaining qualifications

As well as traditional qualifications (GCSEs, A levels and first degrees and post graduates) other qualifications such as BTEC First, National and Higher National Certificates or Diplomas (alternative academic qualifications) or the more 'practical' NVQs, City & Guilds at Levels 1, 2, or 3, OCNs (Open College Network) or special City & Guilds Land Based Services awards.

You may already have GCSEs 0 Levels, and other formal qualifications, but if (owing to your illness, or other reasons) you have not been employed for a long time, there are benefits to studying towards exams again, reasons could include: going to college will help you get back in to the routine of getting up and ready for college, getting used to putting in a hard day's work again, by studying again enables you to refresh your memory of long-forgotten facts, mathematical formulas and so on, and in any event even if you haven't forgotten what you learned at school, college and beyond; unless you only took your exams within the last few years, what you would have learned at time, will probably no longer be on the curriculum, so it's worth getting your Maths, Science, History (or whatever) up to date. Now for some information on a few specific qualifications:

GSCE's and A levels

GCSEs (and 0 levels which they replaced) are standard academic qualifications, subjects ranging from Physics, Maths, Geography, Languages etc (although such exams can be taken in non-academic subject such as Art or Sport Studies). A levels cover most of the same subjects, but in much more depth. It therefore follows that A Levels carry much more 'weight' than GCSEs or 0 Levels when it comes to employment.

BTECs

More 'vocational' than traditional GCSEs and A Levels, (although most subjects are mainly academic). BTEC Certificates are part time qualifications, whereas Diplomas require full time study, and all units must be passed to be awarded the Diploma (although if you only fail a few units you will at least achieve the BTEC Certificate). Subjects available include Business & Economics, Science, Hospitality, Religious Studies, Music or Art & Design. The first Certificate/ Diploma is broadly equivalent to 3 - 4 GCSEs Grade A* - C, The National Certificate/ Diploma roughly equivalent to 2 –3 GCE 'A' Levels A* - E, and Higher National Certificate/

Diploma, is roughly equivalent to the standard of 2 years into a 3 year 1st degree course.

National Vocational Qualifications (NVQs)

NVQs don't involve exams, candidates are subject to Continuous Assessment; and are relevant to specific types of work. They are normally studied when already employed (for instance staff who work where I live study the NVQs - in this instance -generally Health & Social Care -alongside their normal day to day duties). They are awarded at levels 1-5.

OCNs and City & Guilds Land Based Services (formerly NPTCs)

OCNs are available levels: Entry, 1, 2, 3 and 4; courses again involve Continuous Assessment. Subjects Available include Horticulture, Engineering, Health & Social Care, Construction and even (strange as it may seem) Debt Collection. NPTCs are specifically geared to horticultural and agricultural learning both for as standalone qualifications, work-based learning for those already in the industry, or for those at college to supplement their existing studies. Qualifications are available in Pest Control, Horticulture, Health & Safety and livestock, and more. C & G Land Based Services Awards are available at various accreditation levels: Entry level and levels 1, 2 and 3.

Modern Apprenticeships

Anyone aged 16 or over; eligible to work in England and not in full-time education can apply for a modern apprenticeship. These take between 1 and 4 years to complete, depending on level, and combine study with training on the job, working alongside experienced employees. You will gain skills specific to the actual job you are training for. You are paid a wage, and study towards a related qualification (usually one day per week). There are 3 levels in England:

1. Intermediate = 5 x GCSE Pass
2. Advanced = 2 x A level Pass
3. Higher may lead to NVQ Level 4 or 5 or 1st Degree

In addition to work-related skills gained, Apprenticeships can lead to certain qualifications:

- NVQ Levels 2 -5
- Functional Skills qualifications (for example in maths or English).
- A BTEC National Certificate or Diploma or City & Guilds Progression Award
- A BTEC Higher National Certificate or Diploma or 1st degree

Richard Weaver

Chapter 32 - If you have a criminal record

So have I, a long one! As I said in the forward, it hasn't stopped me being recruited by CHOICE CARE GROUP to carry out interesting, challenging, useful and quite well paid work. It doesn't matter even if you only work 1 hour a week on average.

When I volunteered for Sue Ryder, we regular took on prisoners on day release, one such guy (I can't name him - it would breach his right to confidentiality) was nearing the end of a sentence for robbery, and had been transferred from a closed jail, to an open one (Ford) who had an arrangement with the particular Sue Ryder branch I worked for, which allowed inmates on day release to gain work experience (apologies for talking in code -but I have to be careful what I say). If you research the Sue Ryder website, you will learn to about 20% of ex-offenders or prisoners on placement later get a paid position within the charity. Interesting enough, The National Association for the Care and Rehabilitation of Offenders (NACRO) which is a charity that supports ex-offender in finding work welcomes applications for both paid and voluntary work from ex-offenders themselves, some examples of paid posts are shown below:

Retail Tutor	Classroom Assistant
Environmental Trainer	Motor Vehicle Tutor
Functional Skills Trainer	Customer Service Tutor
Senior Tutor	English & Maths Tutor
Business Admin Tutor	Construction Tutor

NACRO also provides education and training, advice on disclosure of records, help offenders recover from drug or alcohol dependency and positively contribute to their communities. An example of voluntary opportunities within NACRO is counselling other ex-offenders. For people who psychiatric patients who have previously been in trouble with the courts DEAL supports all NACRO staff across the whole spectrum of disability (which includes mental illness).

A couple of other miscellaneous points: (1) When applying for a job, with a record, try to obtain character references using professionals, e.g. a reference from a doctor, usually carries more weight than (say) a neighbour.

(2) If you see a key placed discreetly on a job advert, it means the employer is signed up to "NO OFFENCE", another initiative provided by NACRO. Employers who sign up to the scheme do not positively discriminate in favour of applicants with a record (and nor

are they asked to) but they agree to select solely on suitability for the job - not the applicant's past.

Chapter 33 – Applying for paid work

Effectively completing an application form

- Always use black ink and complete all sections in BLOCK CAPITALS.
- If (for instance) you have never previous worked, don't leave previous employment sections blank - mark as N/ A (non applicable).
- As in chapter 32, a reference from a professional carries more weight than from (say) a neighbour.
- If you have a criminal record -be honest, a lack of honesty is something no employer wants. However, try to restrict information at the early stages, as much as possible. Save your explanations for the interview, if offered one.
- The same applies to your medical history (this is dealt with more thoroughly in chapter 34).
- When asked for additional information, state how much you would like the job, and which specific skills you have that make you ideal for the post.
- In hobbies and interests section; state how these are relevant to the post that you are applying for.

Writing an effective job Curriculum Vitae (CV) and covering letter

Although there is no exact 'right' or 'wrong' way to set out CV, here are just a few pointers:
- The CV should be laid out in roughly the same order as a standard job application form (if unsure, use any blank job application form as a template).
- The CV should obviously be typed (no employer is going to be impressed by a hand-written CV).
- Give sufficient information, but be concise (i.e. don't bang on').
- A CV can be /personalised' (unlike an application form) don't embarrass yourself with issues like a criminal record of lack of qualifications, don't lie of course, simply don't include it. Bring it up later, at an interview, if it gets that far, and also (if applicable) explain why you committed the offences; and your attitude to them now.

A covering letter should obviously be typed as well, should brief (certainly no more than 1 side of A4 paper) state your reasons for applying for this specific post (remember the CV should be a generalised document of which you have a number of copies) and again relevance of particular skills, hobbies and interests for a particular job should be stated on the covering letter, not the CV, for the same reason.

Speculative applications

This is when you write to a company enquiring whether they have a vacancy for the sort of job you are interested in. Letter should be brief, but clear (and again typed) and accompanied by a CV.

Telephone applications

If an advert for a job asks you to phone for about a job, check the advert to see whether you are supposed to request an application pack, or to arrange an interview. When the manager, staff member (or whoever) answer the phone start by saying something like "Good morning (or afternoon) my name is X, and I'm interested in your vacancy for ... " and then either say "could you please mail me an application pack" or "Can we arrange an interview at a mutually convenient time?" depending on what the advert specifies.

Interviews

Allow plenty of time to prepare yourself physically (e.g. ironing clothes, cleaning shoes etc, and having a decent meal -the last thing you need at the interview is to have your stomach rumbling, or worse still burping while at the interview) and mentally. Try to anticipate awkward questions the manager might throw at you - for example if he or she sees from your application form that you have two previous convictions for violence, be prepared with answers to tough questions about - you don't want to be put on the spot. Also, have a few questions ready for the manager, it shows you are interested. One very important thing: don't try to calm your nerves by smoking just before the interview - your potential employer won't be impressed by bad breath!

Chapter 34 – When to 'Come clean' about your medical history

As I briefly mentioned in chapter 33, keep details about your mental health issues until later. If you progress to the interview stage, be honest about regarding any ways in which your illness or condition may affect your work, but also remember to point out how you get around such problems (coping strategies), if you are currently in (or have previously been in) voluntary work say to your prospective employer that your 'issues' don't (or haven't) prevented you doing so. Remember to draw attention to any 'strengths' you are endowed with by your illness/ condition (such as my Asperger's endowing me with a naturally retentive memory; that is, I remember lots of facts, formulas, jokes, songs and so on). As I mentioned in chapter 25, anyone with diagnosis can understand and support someone else in a similar situation in a way people who are 'well' cannot. To use this skill certainly doesn't require working in care (although if that's what you want to do anyway, then fair enough). In any place of work it's easier for existing employees with special needs if someone joins the team who is in much the same situation. Also, employees with extra difficulties will probably cope better with customers or clients with special needs.

Richard Weaver

Chapter 35 – Choosing suitable work

For people like me (who have Asperger's syndrome) jobs that are highly stressful are a 'no-no'. Such jobs include police officer, armed forces personnel, fireman or firewoman, airline pilot, teacher doctor, nurse, solicitor/ barrister or working in catering. Admittedly, as I said early on in this book, I have worked in catering - and to be honest, I absolutely hated being 'rushed off my feet'! Work such as horticulture (gardening), computer work, labouring (you will need to be physically fit and strong to do this) or shop work (as long it the shop isn't excessively busy for a lot of the time); is far more appropriate for a person with a diagnosis of AS. If you have Asperger's but not the usually accompanying problem of dyspraxia (poor co-ordination) then jobs such as construction, vehicle maintenance, or carpentry may be suitable (although these jobs will, in common with labouring, require you to be physically fit and strong).

For people with mental conditions that don't include AS, it stands to reason different principles apply. I am in no position to comment on which jobs are compatible with various mental health conditions - my simple advice would be to ask your psychiatrist and other care professionals who understand your issues and know you personally. Nonetheless, here a few general possibilities (I have dealt with mental illness and learning difficulties separately):

Mental Illness	Learning Difficulties
Office work	Cleaner
Carpentry, plumbing, electrician	Sales Assistant
Shop worker/ Manager	Painter/ Decorator
Religious Minister	Carpenter
Bank Teller	Gardener
Cleaner	Labourer

Richard Weaver

Part Eight – Community care

Chapter 36 – Differences between Nursing homes and Residential Care homes

A psychiatric nursing home (as the title implies) provides nursing care for the mentally ill or those with learning difficulties. As much as possible service providers (companies who run nursing or care homes) try to keep these two groups separate. If a resident has learning difficulties and mental illness, he or she would still ideally be placed in a care home with others with LDs. As will be seen in chapter 37 such nursing are normally secure owing the degree of challenging behaviour displayed by service users. Care is delivered by a combination of qualified nurses and support workers. Depending on client need, nurses may be Registered Mental Nurses (RMNs), Registered Mental Learning Difficulties Nurses (RMLDs) or Registered General Nurses (RGNs) or a combination.

A residential care home caters for individuals who require support, on a long-term basis, but who do not need 24 hour, round the clock care and do not display a marked degree of challenging behaviour. In practice, some residents in care homes do have issues with marked or significantly challenging behaviour (and there need staff support when going out) and some will require 24 care, in which case, their funders will pay for a member of staff to be present solely for that person all hours of the day and night. For obvious reasons, this is a very expensive service to fund.

Richard Weaver

Chapter 37 - Which is right for you?

Nursing homes

The Hayes Unit (where I met "Sue", and others) was a secure nursing home for people with a combination of Asperger's syndrome and mental health disorders (in about 2004 its status was changed to that of: Independent Hospital). All exterior doors and on the home were kept locked at all times (and the windows only opened a few inches). The kitchenette, dining room, office and staff area were also locked at all times. The home had a garden (surrounded by a perimeter fence about 10' high) and residents had to be accompanied (or 'escorted' as the staff called it) even out there, and certainly in the non-secure parts of the grounds or beyond. Upon admission all residents' section 17 forms required 2 escorts (sometimes 3). For those admitted who were already subject to a 37/41, they had no leave at all (except 2 to 1 in the grounds) until the Home Office allowed otherwise (this section wasn't controlled by the MOJ at the time). The process of working down from 2 to 1 support through 1 to 1, 'Tag along (unsupported if out with another resident who was) to truly unsupported was a process that took several years. The management were not in the business of taking risks. A few more years building up unsupported leave (plus being allowed out with ever increasing amounts of money) and (if like me,) sectioned for arson; gradually building the trust with tobacco and lighters on me when out alone, and finally you moved on. To my knowledge, there are few, if any, nursing homes for the mentally ill are not secure.

Residential care homes

Although there is no clear legal definition of what "Care" means, in broad terms it relates to support with basic functions e.g. eating, using the toilet, washing and dressing as well more complex (and satisfying tasks) such as cooking, attending college/ going to work, shopping; the open-ended possibilities are numerous.
Whether a particular care home is secure or not depends on client need. People with mental health problems (but not learning difficulties as well) who require secure accommodation will either be place somewhere like The Hayes 'Unit (see above) or detained in hospital. On the other hand people with learning difficulties who need the support of a secure environment are often looked after in care homes with minimum levels of security (for example, the front door would be locked, and a fence around the garden, however the access door to the garden would normally remain open.

For people with mental illness but without learning difficulties (who don't need a secure environment) but do need reasonably high levels of support, they would be placed in 'open' care homes, and except when their illnesses 'flair up' to a dangerous degree, they are entitled to come and go at will (unless on a conditional discharge of 37/41 - in which case the MOJ may impose some limits on leave, and of course the resident would be required to live at the care home as directed).

Chapter 38 – Funding applications

Nursing homes

If you are admitted to a nursing home, the funding will be the sole responsibility of your Primary Care Trust or PCT. The PCT is the local NHS authority responsible for patients in your geographic catchment area (I briefly mentioned this in chapter 3). As the fees for people to stay in places like that are so high (around £400 to £600 per day) and especially with constant Government cutbacks in spending on healthcare, PCTs won't fund such placements unless it is absolutely imperative. Even when this is the case, an application is often turned down the first time around (and even on second and subsequent applications, as the PCT simply don't want to purchase the treatment). In my case, when the application was submitted, a lengthy process followed, including hospital staff and I being required to fill in a questionnaire requiring to me answer a lot very personal questions. After that, the PCT stalled and stalled, and in the end said "Yes it is our responsibility to pay for Mr Weaver's care, but we have no money left", obviously an excuse. In order to get the funding for my placement at The Hayes Unit, my parents had to threaten to sue both the PCT and the Secretary of State for Health if not obtaining the funding (and therefore not getting the help I needed) resulted in me doing something so grossly reckless I either died, went to prison or a maximum security hospital. Only then did the PCT back down. I'm saying all this to warn you how hard it can be to obtain funding (and why), but also to illustrate why it is worth fighting hard to raise funding when it's that crucial, and to remind you DON'T give up!

Prior to admission to The Hayes Unit, I was an in-patient at St Ann's psychiatric hospital in Poole, Dorset; awaiting funding for the specialist treatment The Hayes would provide for my multiple mental disorders and Asperger's syndrome. This being the case I had to undergo an assessment for Continuing Health Care. The law states that if your needs are 'severe' in at least one predetermined area or a 'priority' in any two, on a scoring 'checklist', carried out by a multi-disciplinary team, you quality for 100% NHS funding regardless of financial status.

Many people have, in error, paid £1000s for care the NHS should have funded If you discover (or even have reason to believe) this has happened to you, a friend a relative, a solicitor may be able to help you reclaim the cost. If you do have to pay, you should seek advice about protecting your assets (e.g., your home)

According to literature produced by Farley Dwek solicitors, who specialise in healthcare funding; the entire process of an application for specialist care funding (as in my funding for the Hayes Unit) can be (clients words) "Intimidating, frustrating, unfriendly even adversarial". Believe or it not even Continuing Health Care Assessors themselves have described the process in such terms!

Care homes

You would think, logically, funding for care homes is easier to secure for 2 reasons: (1) the overall cost of the placement will be considerably less than an NHS hospital, let alone a private nursing home and (2) because the funding for care homes is split between the PCT and social services, the cost component for PCT is lower still. Admittedly, if the person is currently in hospital (to which social services make no contribution) if he or she does move in to a care home, social services do now have to pay (the fact that overall cost to the taxpayer is far lower, in the light of various government bodies being very compartmentalised, doesn't, in practice, come in to it).

Chapter 39 - Complaints

If you are not happy with the way a member of staff, management or a fellow resident (or even a visitor or contractor carrying out repairs etc on site) treats you (insulting or swearing at you, stealing from you, or even physically or sexually assaulting you, then you have the right to (and should make a complaint). If the complaint concerns a fellow resident I would recommend you speak to your key worker (if on duty) or allocated staff member for that shift, in the first instance (some care homes do not have a key worker system, in which case your allocated staff member would be the obvious choice -unless you don't get with the staff member) in which case, another support worker who you feel you can trust. If where you live does have a key system and you don't get on with your key worker, I suggest you ask to change key worker without delay!

If the complaint is about a member of staff (or a contractor) you could try resolving with him or her first, but if that fails or if you want to try another route; or if the issue is one of house policy; you will need to take up the matter with a member of management. If management cannot sort the problem out, in a way you are happy with then you could contact an Advocate (see chapter 40) or The Care Quality Commission (see chapter 41) or you could write to a member of management at Regional or Area level or even deal with matter through the civil courts and/ or press charges. Note, on the subject of complaints, although fairly unlikely in practice, staff are quite within their rights to complain about or even prosecute you if you give carry out an act against the staff member of a similar nature.

If the problem is between you and the manager or deputy manager of the home itself you will have either go to regional or management (in short, the company employee, or member of management who deals with your complaint if it involves someone who works for the company, obviously needs to be 'higher' than the person with whom you have a problem. You have the above, other options.

Richard Weaver

Chapter 40 - Advocates

Advocates in the 'conventional' sense are different from IMHAs. Advocates are available (for instance) for people with diabetes, and some branches of Age UK provide an advocacy service. In general, advocates help when you are having problems such as accessing benefits, or services. He or she argues your case for you. In common with IMHAs, advocates cannot act as substitute solicitors or barristers. There are also Advocates who specialise in working with people to whom the Mental Capacity Act applies.

Self-advocacy

You may not necessarily be able to get the help you want first time around and so have to argue your case, complain and so on. If you do wish to complain about something, bear the following in mind:

- Be clear in your mind what you wish to complain about.
- Write details down, before you forget them.
- When sending letter or email, mark it complaint so this is clear to the reader.
- Be sure complaint is addressed to correct body and department.
- Ensure you include address, phone number and email address.
- Be clear, to the point and don't 'waffle'. Bullet points get the message across clearly.
- Always check letter/ email before sending it, and get someone else to do the same.
- Remember, there is often a time limit for dealing with complaints -make sure you don't miss the deadline.
- Although complaints can take quite a long time to resolve, if you think the person you've complained to is 'dragging their heels', don't be afraid to chase them up about it.

When I was at The Hayes Unit for 8+ years, I exercised my right to annual Tribunals. For reasons I've made clear in chapter 4, I engaged a solicitor, however I still prepared a lengthy report on myself for the Tribunal, as well preparing notes for a final verbal "Summary" prior to the Tribunal considering whether to discharge the section.

Also, in various places I've lived (including my current one -the location of which needs to remain confidential) when I am not happy about something I compose a letter to the Manager explaining the relevant facts.

Richard Weaver

Chapter 41 – The Care Quality Commission

The Care Quality Commission sends inspectors in to every care home, nursing home, general hospital and psychiatric hospital in England plus the commission carry inspections on GP surgeries, dentists -in short, practically every branch of the NHS and private care sector. They also oversee social services departments.
The CQC work with The Relatives and Residents Association, as part of their "Tell us about your care" to obtain information from people who use the services, which helps CQC in their work.
CQC claim they have inspected homes all over England, and although they have seen many examples of high quality care, they also, apparently, have noted standards of care fluctuate (vary) considerably from one care home to another, and; more significantly, care homes tend to provide better care than nursing homes. In latest inspection checks (correct 2014) 378 care homes met all required standards, 201 required improvement, and 40 'required enforcement' (very poor).

Richard Weaver

Chapter 42 - The Mental Capacity Act

Definition

The Mental Capacity Act is a law passed in 2005, in England and Wales, empowering carers (family and friends of service users) and health care professionals to make decisions on behalf of those deemed to "Lack Capacity". The term "Lacking Capacity" means 1"An impairment of, or a disturbance in the functioning of, the mind or brain". It only applies to people who:

- Live in England or Wales.
- 18 years of age or over.
- Have a mental illness, disorder or learning difficulty.
- Live in a hospital or care home, lack capacity to agree to be there -when not being there would place them at risk of harm.

Some people's ability to make certain decisions may be impaired permanently because of dementia, a learning difficulty or have suffered a brain injury. Other people, however, may only lack capacity for a temporary period, owing to confusion or being unconscious. Just because someone has a particular diagnosis, or is detained under the Mental Health Act, does not in itself mean they lack capacity.

Before making a decision, the "Five principles" of the Mental Capacity Act must be considered. These are:

1. Assume the person has capacity to make the particular decision, until such times as evidence shows otherwise.
2. Give as much support as possible to help the person make their own decision.
3. Respect the right to make an unwise decision.
4. If a decision is made on the person's behalf, it must be in the person's best interests.
5. Any decision made on behalf of another, should be as least restrictive as possible.

When deciding whether or not someone lacks capacity, includes looking at the complexity of the decision that has to be made. Also an assessment of whether someone lacks the capacity to make even a simple decision can usually be carried out by family or friends, assessment of capacity regarding a person making a more complicated decision; may need to be carried by a doctor or other professional.

It is a common misconception that the Mental Capacity Act is there to 'detain' people in care homes for a brief period, on the same basis as under the Mental Health Act. Whilst it is true that The Mental Capacity is sometimes used to deprive people of their liberty for a short period of time, the legislation (Act of parliament) enables (with some exceptions) almost any decision to be taken on another's behalf. If the decision being made involves the person going out (or permanently leaving) before the person is prevented from leaving the hospital or care home under MCA, a request is must be made by the "Managing Authority" (the care home or hospital where you live) to the "Supervisory Body" (Council or PCT). In order for a deprivation of liberty not only must the five principles be applied but you must also be deemed "Best Interest Assessor", who is not involved in your care and another assessor. A "Best Interests" report will be submitted, which may conclude you should not be deprived of your liberty, or you should be deprived of your liberty, but subject to amendments (changes) to the request by the "Managing Authority" or that the request made by the "Managing Authority" should be granted on the criteria (conditions) the home/ hospital asked for. Under normal circumstances, only a standard application for DOLS (Deprivation of Liberty Safeguards) will be made to the Supervisory body, which can take a few days to process. In an emergency an urgent application can be submitted (although it still has to be backed up by standard application) and such an application can be dealt with practically at once. If the Supervisory body turns down the application, no further action is taken.

If you are deprived of your liberty, staff must follow the codes of practice under MCA. You also must be provided with a representative (Supervisory Body will ensure you are allocated one). If you want to challenge your Deprivation of Liberty you can ask for a review (as can a friend, relative or anyone else who has an interest in your welfare). If your situation changes you will automatically get a review. You can appeal to the Court of Protection.

Chapter 43 - Miscellaneous

Mental Health Act

A person detained under sections 2, 3, 4, 5(2), 5(4), 37, or 37/41 who escapes or absconds, although liable for arrest and return to hospital, the act of escaping or absconding is not in itself an offence. The police, upon arresting a sectioned patient who is AWOL (Absent Without Leave) are not responsible for returning him or her to the hospital, but they are responsible for ensuring the person is returned. The same applies to a patient in the community, subject to a Guardianship (section 7, page 30) or CTO (section 17a, page 31), however in the case of a CTO, may be recalled to hospital and thus resume section 3. A patient subject to any of the above sections who is absent without authority for 28 days consecutively (in a row) is automatically discharged from detention; and therefore no longer liable to arrest.

Special Hospitals

Apart from citing reports from former patients of such places, I have said little else about them. Although some patients I have encountered formerly held in hospitals like Broadmoor or Rampton clearly didn't need to be there, and shouldn't have; many patients detained in high security hospitals of this nature, have been indefinitely detained after conviction for very serious crimes ranging from murder -including killing children (albeit the charge would have been downgraded to manslaughter to avoid an automatic life prison term) to rape, child molesting, mutilation and crimes that would make most people want to be sick.

If you cast your mind back to chapter 4, when I explained the legal definition of a psychopath, it starts to make sense. Of course, by no means are all violent offenders with mental health problems psychopaths, in Special Hospitals, or anywhere else - many suffer from schizophrenia. Contrary to what many people think, schizophrenia is NOT a 'split-personality', in fact the very existence of such a diagnosis is very seen quite dimly by many doctors. Nor does Schizophrenia necessarily involve hearing voices or hearing voices have to mean the patient is schizophrenic. Hearing voices is a symptom of psychosis (a broader term for mental illnesses that resemble schizophrenia). The actual diagnosis means (whether or not it involves hearing voices, 'seeing things' and so on) is that the sufferer is detached from reality.

Ever experienced mental illness or distress?
Are you affected by autism, or learning difficulties?
Or is a friend, relative or your partner having such issues?
Do you have a professional interest in the subject?
Or are you just curious and want to learn more?

In this book these matters are addressed together with rights under the Mental Health Act, Employment, training, studying for A levels or other qualifications, persons with mental health disorders coming into contact with the criminal justice system (including emergency transfers from prison to hospital), how to deal with being bullied because of having psychiatric problems or others trying to exploit such people financially, sexually and so on. This book also looks at placements for people moving on from hospital, ranging from funding to the suitability of the placement for the individual. This book looks at a number of other topics including a number of references to my own 'recovery journey', some of which constitute the odd line here and there, others are more detailed.

Read on...

Lightning Source UK Ltd.
Milton Keynes UK
UKHW041038180219
337530UK00001B/4/P